KALEB SETH PERL

OWN
YOUR
TRUTH

NEW REVOLUTIONS PUBLISHING

Published by New Revolutions Publishing

ISBN-13: 978-1-913816-35-3 (paperback)

First published: 2021

Cover Concept:

Kaleb Seth Perl & Rebekah Yael Nur

Cover Design & Book Formatting:

Rebekah Yael Nur

Copyright 2021 by New Revolutions Publishing

Contact: ksperl@protonmail.com

CONTENTS

PRE WORD

Your truth is that you are not only a physical biological being. You are a part of a much grander inheritance. You are not separated from the Source Intelligence of your Self. It is when you remain within your mind, and you think and act from the minds of others, that you are given a lesser truth. The Greater Truth is within you, for you are a part of it and not apart from it.

It is time to reconnect with the Greater Truth, and this current life experience can be your *means* to do this. Do not allow others to sabotage your own Ark. This material is for the allowance of your own truth to become manifest within your physical life expression.

Do not be fragmented – Be Gathered. Be Whole.

It is time to

own your truth

INTRODUCTION

Truth is not something beyond you. It is everywhere, in all forms. It is present within the mundane as well as the sacred. It is hidden from you because you have been conditioned neither to perceive nor attempt to seek it out. What is referred to as 'Truth' is not complex. Only it's manifestations and partial expressions into physicality have become complex because of the obstacles placed by humanity and others. Truth is simple in that it is your inheritance. And yet humanity has been kept from its inheritance through forms of tyranny, as we have spoken of. There are no 'chosen people' for this inheritance – it is available for all. There is only the effort that each person is required to make in order to gain their own recognition and allowance of their inheritance. The blockages that are placed upon you can be removed by you. We cannot remove them for you.

Each individual is the alpha and the omega – the beginning and end of their own journey. Doors can be opened for you to step through, yet each person must reach to turn the handle of the door. And to take that step.

When you take that step, you go no further than where you already are. And yet something comes to you. You will have made a shift – a realignment. There is no separation between what you are and what you will become for both already exist. It is the recognition and activation of this reality that is necessary. And you shall meet yourself again, and again, and regain remembrance.

For now, humanity must break out from its vibrational shell. And for this, you must do the Work. We have transmitted much in the previous material. This is the preparation to assist in your own alignment. Yet *you need to get to where you are*. You need to get aligned with the truth of yourself. This is the Work to be individualized as well as connected with the Center. No one else can do this for you while you are in physical manifestation. The world in which you live requires that you begin to live your own truths. It may be a lesser walk in the woods to begin with. Yet this Path aligns you with the Greater Way. If there is ever a time for humanity to grow into its inheritance, then that time is now.

It is time now to turn attention away from worldly focus to internal, individual focus. Each individual awareness and experience *can* and *does* make a contribution to the collective. In the following communications, we wish to bring the attention back upon the truth of the individual self.

It is time to move from intention to completion. For this to happen, you each need to learn how to *own your truth*.

PART ONE

'Until you know this deep secret – "Die and become"
- you will be a stranger on this dark Earth.'

Goethe

ONE

There are things which need to emerge within humanity in order to allow for the continuation of this path of evolvement. Certain elements are required from life on this planet. For the most part, these 'requirements' are not always consciously produced by people as they are submerged in a perceptual fog of anxieties, frustrations, distractions, and vibrational imbalance. This contradiction lies within yourselves – as does the way out. We do not talk of overt revolution, for these actions have only gained temporary respite at best. Revolutions have been energetic outbursts that the system has eventually assimilated and fed into itself. A genuine new cycle (a re-volution) is through a shifting of the vibrational patterns and the application of expanded consciousness and cosmic 'co-action.' That is, an increased mergence between the Greater field of consciousness and its localized expression through individualized human beings. This form of conscious mergence and 'consciousness collaboration' cannot take place through unconscious automations – the human robot. For this reason, covert activities have taken place upon this planet to assist humanity overall, and to raise certain 'sensitive' individuals to finer degrees of awareness.

We shall be direct here. Not everyone is expressing their capacity. In this, it can be said, in terms of *inner state,* that not all are expressing equally within the physical lived experience. There are different levels of life expression. For now, we shall say there are three categories, in reference to inner states. Do not confuse this categorization with your social-cultural descriptions for they are not to be mixed. In the first tier, the people are automatons – human machines – and live an ordinary life. They may be office workers, people of religion, politicians, businesspeople, philosophers, and more. These people think that they exist, yet have no *real being*. In the second tier, the people have acquired some form of permanent *being*. These people recognize that there is a Lesser Reality and a Greater Reality. Such people are said to be 'of the world yet not of the world.' These are the people who can, and do, 'make the Work' upon this planet and, through this, assist all levels of evolvement (cosmic, planetary, individual). In the third tier, are those few people who now exist through all these three planes of evolvement and, as such, are not limited to the temporal-spatial restrictions of the Lesser Reality. The aim of the Work is to develop within people the capacity to evolve from tier one, and to exist and function as tier two individuals. From here, it is possible to evolve to tier three. The Work aims to develop the permanency of *being* that aligns with the Greater Reality. It can be said that tier one, two, and three align with the circles of humanity known as exoteric, mesoteric, and genuine esoteric, respectfully.

Within the very core of the human being there is an inherent need to *feel connected*. This essential part of the being lies deep within and has been subdued through many, many years of forgetfulness and external forms of 'intentional forgetting' (conditioning). There has been much activity on all spheres to prepare humanity for the times that are coming, and which are already upon you. Also, there is an increased push for 'intentional forgetting' to be fostered upon the human race. As we have attempted to make clear in previous communications, there is an agenda to 'massify' the human race, and to steer it away from a path of individualization. In this, there is an attempt to increasingly isolate people so that both external and internal relations are blocked. The first phase of this is through a psychological operation. As discussed previously in 'Own Your Sovereignty,' power operates through dividing people at the base of the system. Divide and conquer is a well-known and much used strategy through human history. Power through numbers has been avoided at all costs. For this reason, you may have noticed that mass public gatherings have been increasingly prohibited under various new authoritarian regulations. They do not want for you to gather – to bring together strength in numbers.

The appearance of power always needs to be sustained by the weaker agency. The genuine power that sustains itself, from within, is always the greater force.

Physical human relations within social and cultural settings are also being highly regulated and controlled. This too is a deliberate policy.

There is a long-term plan to keep people from becoming *individualized* and a *coherent collective*. In this, people are being programmed to sustain their individual personas and to act as unruly masses when together. If these subversive measures are maintained, and then assimilated into your societies and cultures, then humanity will find that its future evolvement will be much harder. To speak directly, there is a particular future direction that is detrimental to the essential path of evolutionary life upon this planet.

At the same time, we see much 'triggering' that is occurring across the planet. Crisis moments and critical circumstances also assist to 'jolt' the *being* of the human into increased awareness. Those individuals beginning to open their sleepy eyes, and to perceive what is now happening in this reality, upon this planet, now need to start to *own their truths*. It is time to drop all the falsities that gave you home comforts. Alienation is more and more promoted in your isolating cultures. And yet, alienation is also used by you as a defense mechanism. It is a division, a split, that occurs within the self. Like an island that separates from the mainland, it wishes to find a secure space for itself against the disturbances upon the mainland. By splitting off, it believes it will be safe and secure. This self-isolation may have uses within certain contexts, and for specific time periods only, yet if prolonged it will weaken the 'island.' You are aware of the phrase in your history: 'No man is an island.' In truth, you are each a 'part of the main.' If there is a divide, a separation, then at some point you will fall into this gulf. It will not ultimately protect you.

The controlling authorities are now attempting to re-wire your world – physically and energetically. We, and others like us, are wishing to assist people to re-wire themselves. The Work begins from the inside out, and not the other way around. You – the human being – are the foundation for the future to be built upon. Yet it needs to be developed *by and through you* and not 'over and upon' you.

The human being is not an ideology. Life is not something that should be above you or beyond you. It is *who you are*. The human being is a process, a living path. And yet, there are those in authority that wish to make life into a division – into a separation that can be sustained and controlled. When you see this, it cannot be unseen. Your default is your *being resonance*. It knows not ideology, beliefs, categories, or divisions. The unification must be recognized as your Self, first and foremost.

Humans are turning away from their own unity through fears of being 'in the void.' The unity of being has so many different and varied forms. It does not stop with the end of the physical life expression. And yet, this fear of shifting from the life expression – known as 'death' – is programmed into you as a dreadful final end. This is not so. It never was.

TWO

The 'death anxiety' is a great awakener as much as it is an inducer of fear. It is being used against you, in order to subdue people into obedience through anxiety and worry. The theme of bodily death is now widespread in your societies. The authorities hope that this will be enough to persuade you into submission. It is as more psychological than it is biological. This theme has been utilized throughout your civilizations for the aim of maintaining power. Know also, that the sudden realization of the temporal nature of the life experience can jolt the 'being' into a heightened state of presence. It is important to relate to the life enhancing aspects of living in physicality. As you say, life is miraculous. Do not allow this wonder to become mundane. Your potentiality in life as a human being is tremendous.

Life is a work in progress – this is its beauty. Any force or agenda that seeks to contain, restrain, or inhibit, is anti-life. And in this, it is also against the natural, evolutionary cosmic laws. Unless each person makes a conscious decision of which path they are on, then they are on no particular path. They are the *floaters*. To give an evolutionary analogy, in your primordial oceans, was it the *floaters* or the *drivers* that first made the effort to shift from the waters and onto the land? To shift from one perceptual reality to another takes real effort. It is like breathing a different air. As such, it requires new organs that are *developed through effort*. We say that this requires intention and focused willpower. This is the expression of the inner drive that exists within each person. And this is your truth. When we say – 'own your truth' – we are suggesting that each person takes up the responsibility of their internal heritage.

Your inner strength is your own truth. This cannot be taken away from you. Yet it does need to be owned – and owned by you. It is like an acceptance of all that one has been, is, and shall be: all together in unity. If you venture into the world without your own truth – your own grounding – then you will be swayed this way and that. You may not have the persistence of sustained inner strength to maintain your path. You need to cultivate the capacity within you to create your own pathways in the world. These pathways shall help other travellers. They will also connect in ways you cannot perceive – just as pathways in your brain re-route and re-wire. When making these new connections, new possibilities and potentials are enabled. As can be done within your physical brain, so can you do within your perceived reality. Here, we say again: As Above, So Below.

All changes are connected. No inner shift goes unrecognized, even if it is not acknowledged in the moment. As we have said numerous times, such 'movements' do not occur through a linear framework or time. The linear structures can also act as barriers that hold up the illusion that maintains your own imprisonment.

As human consciousness evolves in its expression, this too shall form new pathways of connections within your vibratory reality. Such a vibratory reality may not be immediately visible to you, yet this does not lessen or invalidate its truth. As it is said:

'There can be no greater foolishness than to deny the reality of something only because one has not experienced it.'

Al Ghazzali

As more and more people express the truth of their consciousness – their conscious awareness – so will more people see this and realize it is the more natural way. To be operating within the false system – within the Machine – is more of a struggle. It is actually easier to walk within one's truth than within the density of falseness. This may appear contradictory because of the conditioning that most people exist under. The social programming makes life appear heavier for you. There is a lightness in one's truth for it is genuine. It is the *essence* of you.

This is not the time now to act frivolous. It is time to see and realize – to perceive – that things of the world are not enough to fulfill the human condition. Do you not see a lack in those who give a misplaced focus onto the ephemeral things that contribute nothing to the path of evolvement? We have called these latest communications as the 'Own Your Self' materials, for humanity has, for so long, been giving away its essential aspects: sovereignty, reality, and truth, as among others. Like a person clearing out their house, and not knowing the real treasures they have, they give them away to passers-by and others, not knowing the true worth of what they give away. This leaves a person's home empty of the true treasure. This creates a longing and a sense of lack within a person. Do not become that person who senses a missing part within their life experience. Do not run with others if you know they are not going in your direction.

There is no visible road map laid out in front of you. The Machine attempts to create an artificial map, and encourages and persuades people to follow their step-by-step guide. Yet we say: follow your own intuition. When you place a foot forward, allow the next step to be taken in balanced relation. Align your steps so that there is a coherency in the actions that you take. Your coherency and consistency will be internal, first and foremost. You may then choose how you wish to present your inner consistency to the world.

Once you have a balanced, internal foundation, then the outer acts will occur in relation to your inner truth – not in relation to external markers. When a person has this sincerity within them, it is easier to walk through the fog of the world. This is part of *owning your truth*.

In your truth there is freedom. We note that so many people have accepted the illusion of their freedom. This is an idea planted within their minds. A person has not achieved freedom until they have gained their personal sovereignty and can experience life without constraint upon the Self. What most people take to be freedom is little more than room to move around within the parameters of the Machine space. True freedom extends beyond the physical body and finds resonance with Greater Reality. If you are not truly aligned with yourself, then it is not freedom. Freedom is also a break from internal patterns that do not allow for moving forward – for evolvement. Things have been made much harder for you than they needed to be. This situation now requires greater effort from you in order to break from these restraining forces. There is truth in saying that humanity has found itself within a loop. To move out of this repetitive loop, incremental changes and shifts need to occur, little by little.

To expand on this, we say that living within this loop has made many people lazy – or, has created a state of laziness that has become attractive for many people, even if unknown to them. This is not solely a laziness in physical terms but a laziness in *being*. A forgetfulness has been induced that permeates far too widely throughout human existence. A person should tend to themselves first – to their own *remembrance of being*. The awakening and sustained awareness of the individual then leads to individualization. Only when new pathways are created within, can there then be new pathways without. That is, a person must first develop the pathway within themselves in order to see this manifest in their outer domain. The external rarely comes before the internal. Do not choose the futile struggle – choose the constructive and meaningful challenge.

THREE

The truth of yourself is in the *seeing*. First it is necessary to clean out all that has been blocking you from seeing this. The cleaning out allows for an expansion of consciousness to flow. If the window you are looking through is dirty, then only a reduced light can enter. Consciousness is to be allowed to enter more fully. Human evolvement is about widening this aperture so that there is a greater range of consciousness to merge with and be expressed through the localized physical body-mind. Humanity is currently constricted within its own space. The oxygen inside your space is constricted, so to say, and this restricts your growth and development. New organs do not develop within you for there is not a recognized need. *You* must provide this need for yourselves – do you see this?

A patient within a hospital, on an operating table, may be provided with new organs delivered to them upon a tray by the doctor. These are physical organs for a physical predicament. Humanity is held within a perceptual predicament. New organs of perception are not 'handed to you on a tray' but must be cultivated from within through an inner necessity. We have spoken on this before. It is a significant point.

We are seeing the crisis points increasing now within your societies. These can be said to be inflection moments. Desirable as well as undesirable pathways are opening up and the Machine is preparing for implementing its desired future pathways. You can be sure that these are not in your best interests. The inner reality is accessed through a *state of being*; the outer reality is accessed increasingly through hierarchy and permissions. Humans also think more and more in such hierarchical ways, and conform to this in their own lives. People react and treat others according to these social and cultural hierarchies. Rare individuals are those who respond to others according to their *state of being*. The more a person lives, reacts, and acts within these confines of hierarchical structures, the less are they aligned with the truth of the self. We suggest that people observe themselves in this. Note when you act from artificial categorizations, constructed and conditioned social norms. These categorizations are going to be more strongly forced upon you now in an agenda to create more social divisions and the break down of pre-existing social relations. Those powers that exert control over humanity are intent on creating divisions amongst the people. This is a strategy to split the masses. The inner being has no division. At the essential core, humanity is unified. There is strength is this unified vibratory alignment. Be wary and careful of those impacts and influences that strive to construct disagreements and schisms amongst you. Do not play their game.

Your truths are not defined by the pyramid of status and acceptance. And yet these structures have established a vibrational realm for you, and many are not aware of this dissonance. The dissonance has become normalized within your vibrational reality. The longer this continues, the more that each generation is conditioned to feed into it. Without knowing, the majority of humanity continue to feed into and sustain their own dissonant resonance. Only by shifting into another direction – another resonance – will you perceive the dissonance in which you have been held. Some people are triggered into making this shift through dissatisfaction; others through recognizing they have a lack within them; other people have an inherent seeking urge within them. And there are the many sleepers who require a greater 'shock trigger' to break the hold of dissonance. As we have said, the 'death anxiety' and the current crises may serve this function. But only with some.

For significant shifts to occur, a threshold often needs to be reached. Is humanity reaching that threshold now? We feel it is so. A realignment can be triggered, and the more this vibrational alignment comes into existence, the more it allows for an increased 'leakage' of the new resonance. What is required are the carriers 'of the message.' That is, the people who hold and transmit the new resonant frequency. This has been happening for some time, amongst certain individuals and groups, as well as established locations acting as carriers. Now it is permeating more amongst the human collective. We would say that YOU are already participating in this – are you not?

Reconnect, recalibrate, and create new pathways – this is your truth now. Each person can participate in this, regardless of where they are physically located. The reconnection is with the stream that, in truth, you have never been separated from – only lost remembrance of. You have always been a part of the 'great flow,' only that so many people allowed blockages to occur, or to be placed upon them. To allow this reconnection, to dismantle the blockages, is now your Work. And this is, initially, an internal and quiet work.

It is a time to take 'time out' from the hectic dissonance of the world in order to refocus, readjust, and realign. The internal space must be a place of balance. It is this balanced center of focus that allows for the connection between individual and Source. A person needs to give themselves the energetic space in which to develop this reconfiguration – this re-tuning to Source signal.

Life is made more complex when too many additions, appendices, and extras are added on. You are sold a constant supply of unnecessary additions that become a part of your baggage in life. This is a needless hoarding. Allow yourself to give space to what is already within you. Stop trying to rent the sequel when you haven't yet seen and appreciated the original film. You need to become your own script and scriptwriter.

There are many 'tools' being sold to you from within the marketplace of the Machine. We ask you: do these one-size-fits-all tools genuinely work for you – or do they only cut-out some of the noise? In this, many people are made passive by so-called tools of well-being that are marketed amongst you. Yet do the tools provide stimulus to activate paths of evolvement within you? There is a well-known saying amongst you: 'to a person with a hammer, everything looks like a nail.' You see how such relations become fixed into a particular reality-set? The truth of a person does not acquire things; does not become part of a 'locked-in' reality-set – it flows like a cosmic wind that blows through and uplifts.

Anything that becomes static is not your inner truth. The terms 'fixed' or 'non-fixed' are alien to the kernel of truth that flows between individual life experience and Source. There is no form in this. Truth has no form.

Only aspects of Truth are perceived to take on the appearance of forms.

Return to the Perceiver – Become the Perceived

Form drops away.

The relationship to oneself is of utmost importance. If you reject a part of yourselves, you will find that you then go on looking for the rejected part in others external to you. This is an endless hunting trip – a never-ending safari of self-delusion. The wish to fix things, and others, outside of oneself has become a trait of the human condition. Few such 'fixers' are those who have first completed the journey within themselves. Many 'teachers' as you call them, are incomplete within themselves and seek compensation through receiving the 'gaze of admiration' from others around them. A genuine guide is not so easily discovered in your societies as such complete people seldom make themselves publicly known. Their physical form exists, yet for them, form has dropped away.

Own your truth by dissolving the heavy attachment to that into which you project the false personality. Leave a residue for the world to see, yet be separate yourself from that residue.

FOUR

What is real to you depends upon the perception bubble that you are encased within. At all times you are emitting a frequency. This is how you are known. Forces operating through the external world have been attempting to increasingly shut down – narrow down – your frequency spectrum over the generations. Sensitive people have often felt this, and from this have felt great discomfort from the ways of the world. In the past, such people shut themselves down, or put themselves away from the world. The feeling-sense of 'not fitting in' can be due to the frequency discrepancy between the individual and the external world. Now we say here: do not shut yourselves down. Do not hide from the world. Do not fight the world either. But do so emit and shine forth your frequency resonance – your vibrational essence – into the world. Your lighthouse resonances are required now. You are bearers of your greatest gift.

A different consciousness reflects a different resonance of being. And it is all around you. There are major transitional shifts coming into potentiality in your current reality. As we say repeatedly, these are frequency resonance changes. What may hold you back is the dominance of the intellect. This faculty was useful in your past survival necessities. Now it is time to move away from the dominance of the intellect for it clings to a particular vibration of logic, linear reasoning, and what you call a 'cold rationality.' Too much reliance upon these mental vibrations will create a mis-alignment with future pathways. We also state here that these 'intellectual pathways' allow a space for other forces to enter and dominate. These are the forces that support the controllers and the systems of the Machine. You can see such intellect-systems coming into strong development in your technologies. They are the pathways of 'cold rationality' that do not align well with the essential resonance of humanity.

Humanity is always communicating among itself, only that few individuals are aware or conscious of this. Humanity has its own resonant communication. Do you see now why there are so many strategies to divide and splinter you? The Machine plans that by creating and furthering social and physical divisions and separation, that this will then affect psychological and emotional divisions that will finally create dissonance and disturbance in your collective resonant frequencies. They are chipping away at the outer clay of the figure, much like a sculptor does, to try to alter the shape (tone) of the whole.

What the human being senses in their relations is a certain energetic within the resonance. Some people have referred to this as a 'soulful connection' or similar. Within and between humanity – as between other sentient beings – there exists and is maintained an energetic resonance of communion. It is *felt*. It is not adequate to put forth here in words. It is an aspect that is felt as a *living feeling*. There is an aliveness in such resonant relations. What we are pointing to here is the Machine agenda to shift to a technologically driven reality on this world. Such resonant frequencies are 'soulless' in the terms you understand, and will serve to greatly alter the vibrational space within your reality. It will be like shifting from multi-color to monotone. If left alone, the planet will naturally realign its resonance. Yet if there is sustained interference and artificial geo-management then this 'hollow frequency' can be maintained here. Under these conditions, it will be difficult for humanity to evolve beyond a certain point. It will be similar to existing within a containment field.

You see here that we emphasize the need to push for moving out of the 'containment pond' and onto new land, such as the early creatures evolving from sea to soil. Humanity is in the process of evolving to exist within a New Land. And this is the land – the space – that needs to be created through you. We may say, in a crude way, that you are participating in a frequency prison break.

There is no truth until you are accepting of self. To live in delusion or self-denial is to be vibrationally mis-aligned with one's Self. Each person must find the honesty to deal with themselves first before they can fully walk the pathways of their own truth. A person is enslaved by their own thoughts, which then create the prison rings around them. If these thoughts are the result of programmed external influences (conditioning), then the individual's prison rings are managed from without and not within. Deep and sincere honesty with oneself is the clearest way to shift onto one's own pathways that are nurtured from within.

Through the lens of honesty, a person comes to realize that the choices they believed they had were only the illusions of choice. The illusion of choice paves the easy path that lies ahead. Each step upon this path is supported by the widespread systems of the Machine. The steps within the labyrinth are easy to take, yet they take a person nowhere. These are the confined spaces that humanity has learnt, over time, to enjoy – or believe they are enjoying. The steps that represent one's truth are more difficult and come with the price of challenge to really accept the deepest space within oneself.

The doorways that tempt you to approach are those on the path of your continued perceptual enslavement. They are wide doors – enchanting, enticing, and alluring. The majority of people follow these roads. It has always been so. Choice upon this planet has always been a matter for you to deal with.

It is not for us to make choices for you. We have never attempted to interfere with your choices. We only transmit communications that may assist in you gaining your rightful clarity of perception. The worlds of freedom and enslavement exist together, side by side. They are not far apart. Both worlds are with you, and there is a fine line between them. The human is conditioned to feel freedom within the reality bubble of enslavement. You think that only to be behind physical bars, under lock and key in your brick prisons, or physically constrained, is to be enslaved. When you are given the space to move around, to participate in your societies, you feel you are free. We refer to this as 'freedom of constricted movement.' We do not perceive this as freedom of the human being.

Due to recent happenings across the planet, we sense that many people are now aware that their freedom was in fact an illusion. There are many more illusions to be revealed.

In owning your truth, you must now take on the responsibility for your purpose. As it is said in one of your gospels: 'The ax is already at the root of the trees, and every tree that does not produce good fruit will be cut down and thrown into the fire.'[1] The human being is the tree. It can choose to bear fruit and fulfil its higher purpose. If no fruit is produced, the tree shall be used for lesser purposes: it shall be used as firewood.

In owning one's truth,

a person steps up to their purpose.

---

1   Matthew 3:10

FIVE

There is great purpose in assisting to bring about a meaningful transition within life on a planet. This is the Work: to participate consciously in the path of higher evolvement. There can be disturbance and much dissonance within these periods of change. The imbalance on this planet in particular is exaggerated due to certain groups wanting to push their agendas of dominance and control. The usual fragility has been heightened and increased due to these intervening and competing forces. These polarizing forces are stepping up in their falsehood as they rely on humans to step back from their own truth. The controlling forces are pushing to implement a platform that over time will isolate the human being from their Source frequency. As we have previously noted, this is like placing humanity within a Faraday cage that isolates the human being from the continual field of resonance.

The Source connection is always inherent as the human being is a localized aspect of this – yet the physical being can be isolated from this frequency. This may be the worst-case scenario.

We have been direct in communicating this. We shall be equally direct to state that there is great support for humanity in these times. Much support is currently outside of your frequency range of perception. Those who can, have more to do to help those who can do less. To be able to do more is itself a responsibility. It is the tree that can bear fruit – to nourish itself and others.

Your truth is the conditions you have in which to Work. Each person has the conditions that they have. No two people are alike in this. It is better to follow one's truth, even if it brings no immediate external merit, than to follow the truth that belongs to another. This has been said in various ways by many of your great teachers of the past. All that has been learnt, gathered, and experienced, now needs to be brought together within you, as a whole. You have gathered the parts – now it is the time to relate them as a unity. Develop a remembrance of the significant moments in life where such empowering lessons were learnt. Bring these energetic memory packets now to your forefront.

Bring to remembrance also any moments of heightened 'peak experience' where your inner self felt enlivened. In remembrance of these moments, you are familiarising your body-mind to the vibrations of those moments. The more that you are familiarized with those frequency patterns, the more your own resonance will recalibrate to these frequencies. This is part of the Work to rewire from within and to establish a new inner home resonance. It is important here not to allow your inner state to wander off into the darker places. If outer circumstances are experiencing disruption and an increase in negative-energy impacts, then establish an inner sanctuary – a refuge of self – within you, where there is a place of high vibration. Fill this space with all your best and most positive memories. Visualize the path of light and joy that takes you away from those darker places.

We understand that some groups and networks have already formed in the physical world through these materials. These are groups that connect together to relate through these communications. It is important that positivity and harmony are maintained in these groups. And, if possible, for an energetic bonding to be established between the participants. These groups and networks also act as 'energy attractors' to assist those in relation to them. If there is a need, use these groupings for sustaining energy amongst you. You have come together because you are like-minded souls, so to speak. Utilize these connections to feel related. Make benefit from them.

Know that this planet is experiencing its own struggle for frequency alignment.

Frequencies also require that they are sustained. So far, many people have been *feeding into* these frequencies and upholding them. Such frequencies will not strengthen further when they are not maintained. That is, when people cease to feed into them. In this, you can take away your energy contribution from those frequencies that do not feed you. Responsibility is upon you to make significant choices in these times. For those reading these communications, there is already a drive to make such choices. As we have always stated, the things we speak of are not for everyone to hear or respond to. Many people are not actively seeking information and material such as this. As such, this information should not be forced upon them. Resetting and realigning is a conscious, voluntary choice. For anything to be forced would be contrary to what we speak of and represent.

Each step is dependent upon the individual. Each person is the center – not any one path or practice is primary. No one glove fits all hands. What is sought external to you should only exist to assist you, not to dominate you. A path or way fits and aligns with you in a mutual agreement. A person cannot transcend what they have not first grounded within them. This is the unity – to be both a 'point in place' and also 'beyond place.' The unity is first a unification within.

A focused concentration of truth can outweigh all the surrounding untruths upon the inward path. This is a focus of sincerity, integrity, trust, and conscious intention. Several individuals with this concentrated focus create a strong vibratory signal. A moment of such truth compensates for years of falsehood. As it is stated amongst some of your spiritual traditions, an hour of focused truth within the self is worth a year of ritual prayer. What you call 'results' do indeed manifest after such focused practices, yet not in the way that many people expect. Again, this is a consequence of the linear programming that has been dominant within your reality. Do not expect tomorrow the harvest of today's Work. And yet, it is also ever-present. Only that the tangible manifestation of it will emerge within 'its own time.' Reality is enfolded upon itself. You do not need to move an inch in order to shift a dimension – yet a vibratory tweak will move a mountain.

Imitation and false work will only deepen the human shadow. The world is already overrun with its shadows. They play out in the politics, the rivalry, the conflicts, and all the other elements that fill your news channels. These are the outer shadows that humanity has cast from itself. They are forced into combat, similar to how the historical Romans pushed their slaves into the arenas to combat the Gladiators and the lions. These slaves were as mostly shadows in contrast to the trained fighters. And so it is now. The new Roman Emperors (the controllers) are pushing the shadows of the enslaved out into the public arena of the world to combat and do battle whilst the proclaimed Emperors watch on, and grow greedy of the prize money.

This Gladiator arena needs to be closed down. The slaves will one day put down their weapons and walk away as free human beings. But first, the Game needs to be known and perceived for what it is. Imitation of the Game has to stop. Do not pick one of their sides, for all such sides are external to you. The human being is not a 'side.' This is part of the entanglement. Once a 'false side' is chosen, then you are in the Game. There is but only Unity in essence. In your mythic stories and modern fables, there is the Dark against the Light. These sides are in battle against each other. And yet, the Dark always came first from the Light. It was the 'fallen' element, as your myths depict. Something 'broke away' and became the adversary. A part of the Light became contaminated, corrupted. See now, that all these are aspects of the same thing. Everything takes place within the Unity.

There is nothing external. The Game is played within itself. When you choose a side, the unity falls away and a different gameboard emerges. But if you focus upon your truth, then you stay connected to the Unity and do not fall upon the gameboard.

You see now how emotions are exploited in this antagonism of the polarity? Polarity is a lesser outward expression of the Unity. Yet it has been exploited within your human reality to deny the Unity.

Dissonance is also a sign that coherence is under recalibration. They work together. But within the perception reality of the Machine, they are at war. Difference has been artificially and deliberately manipulated to oppose the very thing it was meant to support. Difference has been long utilized to create conflict and division when it originally was used to highlight the variation of balance within Unity.

These things show the reality inversion that hypnotizes the human being.

SIX

The human being is human becoming is human *connecting*. The more a person connects through intentionally, the more their signature vibration is established. The truth is always known to the knower. The connection is to be *felt* for it to be recognized. What may be thought to be different connections and communications are really all aspects of the one, same conversation. Like the pure light that enters a prism and is then separated into the various shades of color upon exit. So also, the unified connection is diffused into all different colors once it enters into your reality. Your normal sight and thinking perceptions grade these colors as red, blue, green, yellow, and the rest. You note these are 'separate colors' when in truth they are differing degrees of vibration from the original Source vibration of the pure light. Humanity is immersed within these colors now and misses the underlying unity.

Colors can be mixed together, and a vast range of hues and tones can be created. This is the wonder of the physical life experience. These are the *blendings* that create the diverse manifestations within life.

It has been detrimental to humanity that a small group of people have been persuaded to lord it over you as the 'dominant painters.' They have chosen only to use a very limited range of colors with which to paint the life picture for you. They paint thus: life is like this; the planet functions like this; Nature operates like this; the cosmos is like this and not that. All these restrictive and childlike perception sets have constructed a limited bubble of life for you. Your inner truth knows the falsehood in this. Whilst many upon this planet are being pulled further into these constructed illusions, there are more and more people who are sensing the unnaturalness of this.

To access more, you first need to work with what you have in your current reality. The tools to break out of your reality confinement are here with you. The more you push inwardly for expansiveness, the more pathways will open up. All life participates within a cosmic reality of mutual relations. There are truths upon all levels, upon all paths – and these expand as the paths of perception expand. As you continue to walk upon them, they widen before you. If you walk the paths of others – the programmed paths – then you walk within the measurements others have set. We hope this makes sense.

Our communications are gathered into several books. Yet in truth we are only communicating one book – and that book is YOU. The manifestation of life is this same diversity: the same thread is experienced in different weavings. If you can experience this personally, within yourself, then you no longer need to rely upon external information that is provided by those with their own agendas. They are feeding you a drug. False intoxication diminishes your capacity of being. There is a well-known tale on this; here is one version:

A group of people all happened to die at the same time in some tragic event, and entered the afterlife together at the same time. They were surprised at first to find that the afterlife seemed very much like the life they had known. Soon, entertainments were provided for them. They were treated to all their wishes and desires. They met with others in the afterlife who informed them that this was the Hell that was spoken about previously.

Again, the group of people were surprised for it did not seem anything like the Hell they had been told about. Here, if they wanted to have exciting experiences, they were provided for them. If they desired satisfactions, wealth, celebrity – all desires were fulfilled by the willing custodians and institutions of Hell.

Demons were present also – although they did not look like demons at all. They came with smiles and 'thank yous,' and 'yes, of course.'

Yet, after some time, a day arrived that was known as 'complaints day.' Several of the people in this group went to one of the controlling demons and said:

'We have a wonderful life. We have parties, riches, and lots of excitement and diversions. But we have also noticed that we seem to be withering away. And, little by little, we are becoming unattractive to each other. We are also losing some of the memories of before that once came to us so easily. Some of us are beginning to forget who we are.'

'Yes', said the demon, with a friendly grin, 'Hell, isn't it?'

The vibration of forgetfulness is quite dominant within your current reality-set. It is this which has, over long time, misdirected the human being's inner gaze. Your truth is to bring this back into alignment within you.

When the correct pitch is reached, its sound waves reverberate outwards into the surrounding atmosphere. If there are a sufficient number of these sound waves – the right pitch – moving outwards, then entrainment is produced within the realm.

Visualize a house that was once full of wondrous furniture and beautiful tapestries and hangings. It was a place of harmony, contentment, and happiness. But then a small group of landlords assumed control of the house and devised a new system of rent payment. These landlords were mean and knew that their type of rent payment would not be paid; or the inhabitants would not take them seriously, especially if they remained within a house of wonder. So, the mean landlords devised a plan. It was a plan that would need time, much patience, and yet it was dastardly. They planned to gradually remove all the beautiful furniture, tapestries, and hangings from the house. If they did this over a long period of time, the inhabitants would not be likely to notice - especially if distractions and diversions were provided in the house. And so it was that during the house distractions, the landlords arranged for the contents of the house to be removed. With the contents removed, the ambiance of the house changed. From being a place of resonant, harmonious sounds, it gradually became an echo chamber. Further, the landlords discovered that if they piped in music to each room through a hidden speaker, then this music would echo and reverberate around the whole house. There was no getting away from their particular vibratory sound.

Yet within the inhabitants there had been a small few who had retained their memory of how the house used to be. Through careful observation, and without raising suspicion, they recognized what was happening. They got together and decided to form a guild – the Guild of Chime Makers. They began making chimes that they would carefully hang in different rooms of the house. And yet they would disguise the chimes as something else. One was a standard chair that people could sit on. Another was a seemingly ordinary picture that people could visit and look at. Another was an unusual doll's house that seemed of unique design. And yet the Guild of Chime Makers had persuaded the mean landlords that the children of the house needed a doll's house, and it would help to keep them occupied. The Guild invented all sorts of 'reasonable' explanations for why the landlords should allow them to place their objects around the house – for the landlords did not know that these objects secretly functioned as chimes.

Next, the Guild of Chime Makers decided to train their descendants to become the Guild of Musical Instrument Makers. The later generations created musical instruments which, they said in public statements, fitted in exactly with the type of piped music that the landlords were putting into the house. For this reason, the landlords accepted and tolerated the Guild of Musical Instrument Makers so long as their instruments sang to the same tune as their droll, monotonous music. And so it was. And yet, the

Guild of Musical Instrument Makers also placed a special function into their instruments that allowed them to play a special tone that would resonate with the chimes that they had placed around the house. Once again, the Guild of Musical Instrument Makers placed their varied instruments around the house, dotted in various rooms.

Next, the Guild of Musical Instrument Makers decided to train their descendants to become the Guild of Musicians. This Guild of Musicians began to slowly, quietly, and under the guise of 'doctors of specialist ailments,' to train selected inhabitants of the house how to play and operate the musical instruments that their ancestors had left around the house. As more and more of the inhabitants learnt to play the secret chords of the musical instruments, these sounds resonated with the chimes that had been previously left around the house and, slowly, over time, a new vibration began to flood the house.

Next, the Guild of Musicians decided to train their descendants to become the Guild of Singers. As everyone knows, almost anyone can be trained to become a singer, if they put their heart and will into it. And do you know what songs they taught? They secretly taught songs that resonated with the music of the instruments that resonated with the vibration of the chimes – disguised as popular, bawdy songs, so the landlords would not complain. And do you know what is happening today? The house still exists, yet it is filled with singers who are visiting the various rooms of the house – some of them are choosing to stay in these other rooms – and they are quietly and secretly singing their songs that match with the tone of the musical instruments, which resonate together with the vibration of the chimes. And, gradually, a new song is emerging all through the house.

Will you look for the Guild of Singers, and asked to be trained in the Song of Songs?

SEVEN

To seek for your truth, and to own it, is a responsibility, not a luxury. Time is also both a responsibility, and a luxury, that is seldom available in the way that is thought. The distractions that are constantly provided for you also take you away from *living essentially*.

We observe that so many people live their life experience in a way that we would describe as – on the periphery. Like bathers who are all seated around a pool: watching their screens, playing with each other, having fun, eating and drinking. And yet only a few ever feel the urge to step closer to the pool and to take a look into it. For what would they see? They would gain sight of their reflection.

With outer reflection, comes inward reflection. With inward reflection comes realization. With realization comes responsibility. With responsibility comes *action* and *being*.

With 'being here,' comes an understanding that physical life exists within a realm of time. To understand your responsibility, first grasp the importance of *your time*.

Here is a story to illustrate:

> Like most businesspeople, time is money. One goes with the other, like day and night. And like many tales, this one starts with a dream.

> On one hot summer night a CEO of a large corporation had gone to bed after a tiring day of international business negotiations. All day she had talked with her subsidiaries across the world, squeezing them down on their profit margins, as it was her job to do so. On this night she had retired to her room feeling very sleepy. She fell asleep as soon as her head hit the pillow. Yet soon something awakened her.

When she opened her eyes, she saw a huge shadow standing by the side of her bed. She instinctively knew, with the whole of her being, that this apparition was the Angel of Death. It had come to claim her; to rid the CEO of her mortal body. She could feel her heart pound so deeply that she thought she would die there and then of a heart attack. The Angel of Death began to move away from the bed, and the CEO was compelled to follow it. It took great inner strength but finally she was able to find her voice.

"I'm not ready to leave," she managed to say. The CEO begged and pleaded to be allowed to remain. The Angel of Death stopped and turned to look at her. The figure did not move.

"Let me stay here and I will give you half of my fortune," pleaded the CEO, who was an extremely wealthy person, and used to getting her own way - usually by paying for it. Yet the apparition shook its hooded head. The CEO became quite desperate, her whole body was covered in sweat.

"I will give you all my fortune – everything. Let me remain!" cried the CEO. Again, the apparition shook its head, yet said nothing.

"I will give you all of my fortune for just one day more!" Nothing. "I will give you everything I have in this world for just one hour more!" The CEO was down on her knees, begging. "For one minute more!" "Oh, for the love, for just a few seconds more!"

This time the apparition appeared to nod. The CEO had a few seconds reprieve, and in that moment she felt an immense gratitude for life. Life was the most bountiful of gifts. For just a few seconds more it tasted sweeter than the most exquisite nectar. The CEO ran to her desk and scribbled a few words.

The next day the cleaner found the apartment empty, and the CEO was nowhere to be found. Yet upon her desk was a hastily scribbled note: *Don't waste your time. My whole fortune could not buy me more than a few seconds...don't waste yours...'*

EIGHT

The owning of your truth is not the same as seeking to gain benefit for self. If only self-benefit is sought, then this creates its own imbalance. The sun does not shine for its own benefit; and yet the sun has reached its own truth. All self-truth is unique and yet related in Unity.

As within the human body, each organ has its own truth – its own function and responsibility – and yet also relates to the balance of the whole. All is intertwined and cannot be measured. It is the 'cult of measurement' which has dominated so much of human thinking in past years. Love amongst you and for one another is measured. Gratitude, gain, benefit, necessity, worth, and all the rest – these are all so much measured and valued by calculations in your industrialized societies. When a person is asked to do something, they often calculate and evaluate the worth of it – how much is it 'worth' to them to do it? You see the division in this?

The reciprocity of relations, which are in flow, have been separated into invented categories of measurement – and this all creates blockages and stoppages in the flow. The cosmos does not calculate and evaluate the worth in its integral relations. There is a natural, organic balance in the giving and receiving of energies. This is what has been termed by yourselves as the 'music of the spheres.' Music has a harmony and playful engagement. It can be said that the physical and energetic universe is in play amongst itself. You see: truth is also playful. It is not all seriousness, heavy steps, and woeful burdens. There is a lightness to it also. Many wise people amongst you have expressed great laughter and joy. In fact, some wise people never stopped smiling and laughing throughout their entire lives. We are not suggesting this, however. One person's laugh may be another person's smile. And one person's smile may be another person's inward reflection.

Do not let the pathway of truth become a trail of misery. The realization of your predicament is not amusing. On the contrary, it may bring an initial shock of panic. This is just the first breath. For if you can grasp the context of the situation you are in, you can likewise understand the vastness of the potential and possibilities. Each life experience has a physical duration. Just as there are possibilities during, there have been possibilities before and will be after. Do not feel trapped by the awe of the situation in the physical incarnation.

The more an individual sees within, the more they are able to grasp the complexity and vastness of what lies outwards and beyond. The great expansiveness is in correlation to which you are a part – within which you play a part. As we all do. It is as a symphony, all notes interrelated and playing together. As we said previously, not all voices sing the same note at once, but are to be in alignment. Within this Symphony Hall there is at present a disturbance, and the orchestra has momentarily lost its rhythm. There is a rearrangement taking place, and a swapping of 'musical chairs,' so to say. When the orchestra is once again seated, and begins to play, those with their own instrument of self-truth will be compelled to step forth. In these times, consider that you are learning to tune your instrument. Do not be dismayed that you are making wrong notes, or 'messing it up' a little. This is all part of the reorientation back to one's home rhythm. Attuning to one's home resonance affects others too, although they may not consciously realize this.

We ask you: do you remember the smell of your grandmother's home cooking? This is a residual remembrance that a young child stores within them. Many, many years later they may be in someone else's house, or in a restaurant, or out walking, and this smell comes to them. Immediately, their center of memory – a place of *being* – recalls this 'smell vibration' and relocates them to this place, time, and sense-memory. The child, now a grown adult, can re-live a past experience and bring it forth into the present. Vibratory memory-signatures can be passed along from one to another. A friend might spend some time in your presence and may have attuned in a certain degree to your resonance. They will then take this 'memory-signature' away with them. When they next encounter a similar resonance, they will respond to it more easily. Or, if they are visiting a particular place of like-resonant energy, they will quickly attune to the energy of the place, and benefit from this synchronization, because they have been pre-tuned from being in your presence. These aspects are not readily visible or known, yet they occur more frequently than is realized. More importantly, they *do* function.

There is a popular spoken phrase of contemplation that people use: what is the sound of one hand clapping? We ask: what is the sound of a musician without their instrument? For the musician is you; and the instrument is your own truth. Without these two in alignment, there is no 'music of the spheres.' Many people are not even aware that they are out of rhythm. For them, there is no beat. There is not any background melody.

Yet those who resonate with these communications know – *feel, sense,* and *hear* – that there is a melody.

That there has always been a melody throughout the existence of life.

This is the longing for the origin of song that has kept your inner being in contact with the memory-signature.

Do not be in fear, or have anxiety, over the false, manipulative 'song vibrations' that the Machine broadcasts across your societies. These sound vibrations will not affect you in the same way as others for you are not attuning to them. You may walk through them and not be corrupted. Just like the doctor who demonstrates their inner self-belief and can walk amongst the infectious patients and not be corrupted by the same disease. Maladies, and diseases, need a like-vibration to attach to. If you have fear, then you are offering these maladies a 'lifeline' to attach to. If such energies do not sense an attachment to you – a lifeline – then they will seek this elsewhere.

Many humans unknowingly create their own contamination for they express the fear programming that is given to them. This fear vibration emanates and attracts the maladies of like-resonance. This is like people who are walking all the time with their gaze fixed down upon their feet. How can they perceive anything but the cracks on the floor? How can they expect to perceive the vastness of the road ahead that lays before them if they are focused only upon the cracks?

This journey you are upon is like a caravan moving through the desert. It is a long journey, and the days can be hot and the evenings cool. The desert is vast and stretches long before you. The destiny that exists beyond the horizon cannot yet be seen for there is only sand. The horizon remains sand for many days, weeks, months, and longer. Yet the caravan moves on for it has its own orientation. The lead camel driver has a map of the desert handed down to him by his ancestors. The routes may change, yet the Path remains. The camels that have chosen to be upon this caravan do not fall or lose their footing in the desert for their eyes are focused upon the way ahead. They do not need to look down at their feet for they have seen and realized what is coming. Their steps are guided by this inner sense. The camels stay focused and look ahead. Despite the hot days and the cool evenings, they are sure that one day the caravan will reach its destination – as have the caravans before them.

First, each camel must *own their truth.*

NINE

There is much psychological stress and mental anguish current within human societies across the planet. These stresses are being heightened by deliberate measures. There are greater strains on underlying human relations that are part of the Machine's divide and rule agenda. It is easy to get pulled into these antagonisms. We have stated repeatedly that this is playing 'their Game.' It takes an inner force to take the decision to step back from these external antagonisms whilst remaining within the thread of human relations. To close down pollution from negative vibrations does not mean closing down relations with life. This is the balancing act – of being immersed within the human life experience whilst not attracting the energies and vibratory impacts that are unwanted. This depends on your own *state of being* to be able to walk amongst the world while not being pulled into its unwanted entanglements.

The human life experience requires engagement and participation. This is being the 'particle' and the 'wave' simultaneously. There is not one or the other. Also, to be watchful and self-observant, for it only takes a split second to slip out of your own synchronization. It can take much inner work to reach a state of observant calm – yet it can be toppled in a moment if one is negligent to the hostile forces. It is necessary to recognize one's own place of rest. It is not a place of inaction, but of non-entanglement. In this state, vital energies can be preserved, and their leakage stopped. Human beings 'leak' a great amount of their energies unknowingly. It happens that only a little of the essential vital energy is preserved for the immediate needs of the individual.

This is also the case on the grander scale of the evolvement of human civilization. We sense that these times require a 'rest period' for humanity to step back a little and to realign itself before moving ahead. There is coming a time of great acceleration that will bring forth many new discoveries and advances for your civilization. Yet if you enter this phase as an unbalanced and misaligned collective civilization, further imbalances and fracturing are likely. Consider the preparations of an athlete. Before commencing an intricate series of moves, or a period of intense precision, a moment of rest is taken to prepare the athlete's body and mind. The athlete focuses, visualizes, and works through the coming moves before making the first step. This is where we sense humanity is now at. At this resting point, much internal work can be done – individually and collectively.

Do you realize you are within this resting point right now? Perhaps you do not recognize it as so, for there is much disturbance in the outer world which seems contrary to this. In the world at this time there is going on much of what you call 'soul searching.' There are a great many people now reassessing their life experience, their life priorities, and their relations with others, the world, and the grander scheme. The question of the human being as the human *becoming* is now more at the forefront than previously. Our communications have brought attention and observation onto this subject.

As in all rest periods, there are unnatural forces that seek to exploit this moment. Such forces are rushing in now, backed by the long preparations of the Machine, and other controlling entities. Yet, we say, that humanity has also been in long preparation. Humanity is not always externally manifesting during their time of preparation. Preparation is undertaken often in the privacy of one's own *inner homeland*. When the moment arrives, an external expression can come forth. This can be illustrated by the following:

Once upon a time, there was an Emperor who was extremely fond of roosters, and so one day he commissioned the most famous painter in all his realm to paint him a picture of a rooster. The painter replied that it would take him three years to accomplish this. The Emperor was rather annoyed, but in the end he agreed.

When the three years came to an end, the Emperor summoned the painter, but on seeing that he was empty-handed impatiently demanded: "What about my painting of a rooster?" The painter remained perfectly calm, took up a piece of paper right where he stood, and started to paint. The brush flew across the page in precise and intricate movements. With apparent ease, he produced the lifelike image of a rooster, capturing its very essence. It took him less than three minutes to complete. On seeing this, the Emperor was furious and could be patient no longer: "Have you been deliberately deceiving your Emperor? Is this some act of rebellion? It took you just three minutes to paint that picture; why did you make me wait three whole years?" To which the painter replied: "Sire, first please calm your fury; and when you have done so, follow me and see for yourself."

The painter led the Emperor to a large house and opened the door, and on looking inside, the Emperor realised that the house was filled to the roof with sketches of roosters. Then the painter spoke: "These are my efforts of the last three whole years. Without those three years of work and preparation how could I possibly have produced that perfect rooster for you in less than three minutes?"

This is an illustration of the Work. We suggest that this is the time now for increased inner work. When external travel is restricted and less available, this makes for more travel through the *inner homeland*.

Humans in general are very focused on action and wish to be seen to be active or 'doing something.' In your values, making action is seen as a merit. Those who sit still, or contemplate, are considered as not contributing to your societies. This is but one example of the limited perceptions employed through your conditioning. An individual who owns their truth will know when it is the right moment to act, and when to refrain from action. Refraining from action is not inaction – it is paused action. Such rest periods can be utilized as a time for replenishment. It is a shift in the overall rhythm. As such, it allows also the grander vibratory rhythm to realign and prepare for a new symphonic phase, so to speak. The planet also benefits from these periods of rest and realignment. Many planetary systems are likewise replenished.

You will have noted that there are forces not allowing some of this replenishment to take place. The misaligned and controlling forces are pushing through in order to push ahead. Theirs is a damaging strategy. These forces do not grasp the *resonance of belonging* as you do. Their anger and frustration also stems from this recognition that they feel 'not at home.' The aligned human being feels at home on this planet, even if they may feel less comfortable with their current reality structure. The individual who is connected to their essence, and Source, knows they are always *home*.

The controlling forces will want to bring you too into their sphere of anger, and frustration. The further these forces move away from their own state of being, the more they will feel envious of you. They will attempt not to show this. They will even deny it to themselves, and their self-denial only fuels their own frustration. They will not admit it to themselves: they envy the true human being who is at home with their own self. The person who is not at home with themselves will always be sleeping on the sofas of others.

Your power is to know yourself and how to belong to oneself.

In owning yourself, you own your truth.

TEN

How an individual synchs-up with themselves will determine how they synch-resonate with the larger vibratory fields. That is, the antenna needs to be in tune in order to pick up the signal. That is why we always have stated that everything begins with you – the localized individual.

Whether a small drop or a big splash, the *essence* of the vibration remains the same. The only difference is in the distance of the ripples. The cosmos and the individual are related, energetically entwined. Shouting louder will not enhance this connection. The cosmos hears a whisper the same as a shout – if you are on the same wavelength. When you call to an animal, it responds to your tone, not the language you use. The possibility for communication and the potential for response is based on resonance. The possibilities and potentials, likewise, are within the individual and can be brought forth into the field of perception, and then manifestation. You cannot bring forth what you first do not perceive. This potential is present, yet it has been placed out of view for people have been greatly distracted from themselves. The individual energy has become splintered, and these splinterings of energy are then directed into first one thing and then another. The mass public sphere has become a field of energetic sparring similar to a medieval field of battle.

We say, take back your sword and disentangle from the public wrangling. Know that you are within an energetic ocean. Its ecosystem is complex and is much more than just the rise and fall of the waves upon the surface. These waves are what the limited observer sees. The vast and complex integrated ecosystem beneath the surface is where life exists and expresses itself. During a storm, the ocean waves can be furious. They can sink boats and destroy those who venture forth. Yet beneath the waves, the center of the ocean is calm. There is an amazing array of life and living interaction. If you only stay focused upon the rage and fury of the waves, their rising and falling, then you shall miss the intricacy, inventiveness, and the inner pathways of the ocean.

Likewise, if a person sees only the conflicts upon the surface of the planet, they shall miss the beauty within the hearts of the people and their intricate lives that bind together an immeasurable species.

The place of rest is like the center of the ocean. Over time, each droplet from the ocean center will eventually arrive upon the shore. This is the movement of life. Evolvement is what happens when you reach the shore. Each resting period precipitates its own moment for coming back. Each wave upon the shore brings new droplets, particles, and grains. This process does not rely upon time but rather on rhythm. There is a pattern in such a rhythm. As human perceptions evolve, more of these patterns will become discernible. As these patterns are understood, greater participation in their design can occur. Until that time, those who truly perceive the patterns remain few. Yet such 'pattern perceivers' do exist amongst you, have always done so, and continue to assist humankind along its pathways.

Those of you who have resisted the temptation to go along with the mainstream – to 'blindly follow the masses' – have remained more in resonance and synch with this greater rhythm. This rhythm guides you; often in ways you do not understand or are conscious of. Odd instinctual decisions and inner 'gut feelings' have driven you along certain pathways. In many moments, these intuitions have been followed and they altered the course of your life. This is you following the guidance of the resonant patterns and the greater rhythm.

You cannot expect others to understand or to follow your way – but you can keep to your place on the path. But this too requires periods of reflection; to assess for readjustment and realignment. These are your own personal resting periods. Do not be hesitant to take them if you feel they are necessary for you. It is always a good idea to re-evaluate where you are - both with, and within, your Self. This is your own rhythm and needs to be recognized by you. Each person has their unique resonant signature. This is your true 'identifier' – not your life-given name, or the things that your personality has acquired.

A person cannot outrun their own rhythm, or dance to another's. The cosmos knows you from your own unique vibratory signature.

People often make it much harder for themselves than needs to be. It is as if they try to outrun their shadow, or to detach from their voice when they are speaking. The short-cuts often take you further away from yourself and from your own truth. You need the rest as well as you need the run. A perpetual runner will eventually drop down and die from exhaustion. Energy needs to be conserved for the later laps.

Step back and see yourself within the larger picture. When this can be grasped, then the more intense moments of the life experience can be better understood and accepted for what they are. How many times do you look above you? When you are seated at home, at work, or in your habitual location – how many times do you stretch your head back and look directly upwards? The human being tends to look ahead of them, or to the left and to the right; or, as is often the case, down at their feet. Yet few people look directly above them. Your world will appear larger the more you look above yourself. And so also it is for reality perception. The more you can perceive beyond your conditioned reality programming, the grander you experience your reality.

It is time to gather yourselves together. Not necessarily physically, but energetically. For it is from a coherent, concentrated, and focused point of gathering that one can better reach forth. And it is by reaching forth from oneself that new pathways are created, inwardly and outwardly. Step within – go forth. Step within – go forth. This is the rhythm of life. This is the rhythm of the oceans. It is also the rhythm of the cosmos and the universes. There is contraction, followed by expansion. There is gathering, followed by reaching forth. There is inaction, followed by action. There is rest, followed by movement.

These are not secrets that we communicate. All that we relate can be observed also by yourselves. If humans stopped racing to name, categorize, and acquire everything, they would see, sense, and perceive all these natural rhythms, as did your ancestors. Yet your ancestors were not over-stimulated, as you are today. They had 'space' in terms of spatial perception – yet they lacked the critical perceptive faculty that humans possess today. Humans can today grasp and analyse what they perceive. And yet, so much stimulation and distraction are thrown at you that you do not know what end is up, or even what is real. This can be confusing, and indeed is deliberately made so. The result is that avoidance of such perceptive potentials is preferred by the many. It is 'too much work' to retune the lens of perception – is it not?

It is easier to believe the lie than go in search of the truth. Modern life has programmed a new level of laziness into your so-called 'advanced societies.' People would rather hear about it in the media than consider it deeply. Too many false short-cuts have been provided – intentionally by your controllers – to disengage you from seeking the truth of meaning and purpose in your lives.

We ask:

What is your purpose?

What is it that drives you?

What gives you meaning?

Are you content?

If you continue to seek for the Big Bang, then you have been sold a lie. If there is no Big Bang, then you may think that you have missed something. This then brings you disappointment, and then sadness. And yet: how can you miss yourself? You are standing where you have been standing all the time. It is your attention that has been misdirected all along. If there is a bang, then it is within you. And there need not be any explosion or loud sound, for the truth within works through you in silence.

Enjoy your silence - do not be afraid of its presence. Do not be sold on the lie of boredom. There is no boredom in the Self. Why seek for noise when the silence within speaks loudly?

The noise of the mind-maze is increasing around you. There is no point in adding more to it. Do not give your keys to the jailor. Do not forge the lock that is until now only in your minds. Be free from *their patterning*. Align with your own. There is no need to tie the knot yourself.

Freedom is in the realization of it.

ELEVEN

In our previous series of communications – 'A Revolution in Human Becoming' – we spoke more about the external systems of conditioning, of the Machine, and of the perceptual prison that enslaves you. In the books of the 'Own Your Self' series, we have focused more on the individual, and the inner world of the human being. There is a difference in emphasis, energetics, and tone – yet they are inseparably connected. They are integral, whole, as is the human being and its environment. Everything is connected.

In this reality in which the human being is immersed, it is considerably difficult to find a perspective that is not influenced and affected by your conditions. That is, it is a rare thing to gain a clarity of perception of the ocean when you are swimming in it. The rights and wrongs that have been established are the currents of the ocean. The inhabitants of the ocean ride them, although they do not apply for those who are upon the land. It is the nature of your reality to convince the participants – the 'players' – that their reality is for all. The seriousness of your predicament is a seriousness within your particular reality experience. The truths of your existence are not singular. There are the relative truths related to your life experience as a localized individual expression within this reality. There is also the truth of your *essential Self* that exists simultaneously beyond your reality immersion. When these truths can be brought into alignment, the nature of your reality and the life experience become clearer to you.

Part of this knowledge-experience is to learn how and when to let go of the things in which you cling so tightly. Many swimmers are convinced they are also drowning at the same time, and so they seek out every scrap of driftwood to cling to. This is your human survival mode. Imagine the many fish of the ocean simultaneously thinking that they are drowning. If the fish is always believing it is drowning, it is unable to focus on swimming to any destination. It swims around in circles, stuck in the perception of a survival need. The undercurrents of the ocean are a natural flow. The wise fish know how to connect with these undercurrents and how to 'ride the ocean' with them, expending least energy. Those fish that are distracted by the debris discarded or thrown into the ocean will forever be swimming after jetsam and flotsam. Yet inside the magnificent ocean are great currents in constant motion, taking those fish who learn to let go on an incredible journey.

The fanciful items are on the surface of the ocean. The truer experiences are to be found in the depths below. The ocean is your own meeting point. At every strata of depth, new marine life is encountered. Each stratum has its own ecosystem of life and perception. As a fish enters a new stratum and spends more and more time there, it becomes acclimatized to the new depth – its heat/cold; its fellow beings; the depth perceptions; and the new ecosystem of oceanic relations. The fish closer to the surface know nothing of these depths nor the range of creatures there, for they are fearful of and occupied with the surface predators.

In these deeper strata, new pathways and connections are established. Relations are reshuffled, and the mind patterns are re-wired. A different consistency of consciousness is operative at these depths. The fads and trends of the ocean are being ridden out upon the surface. The essential nature of life in this ocean is discovered within its depths. There is nothing fancy about living deeper within the ocean. The need for fancy and momentary excitement are left behind – there are more magnificent wonders below.

The fish near to the surface will say all kinds of things to distract attention away from the ocean beneath. Stories will abound amongst the fish about the 'crazy ones' who dwell below. The 'crazy depth dwellers' have gone mad from the pressure, they will say. They have strange relations among themselves. They are trying to escape from the real life of the ocean, it will be said. The big song and dances are being played out among the rolling waves, where the storms gather and thrash against the ocean surface. Some ocean laws will try to persuade the fish that it is obligatory to jump into the storm waves and sacrifice oneself for the good of their ocean community. It is a sure route to ocean prestige and fish martyrdom, they will say. Different schools of fish even create their own surface tournaments to see which schools are 'better fish' than the others. This often develops into intense rivalry among the fish schools, and then invented hatreds. Some of the fish schools even do battle against one another. In these, many fish die and become fish-food for the predatory birds that swoop in from above and snatch away the floating bodies. Some fish have even come to suspect that the fish school feuds are deliberately fabricated by the 'birds from above' as a constant food source for them. But these fish are quickly ridiculed for their silly ideas and sometimes banished from the popular surface sea areas.

And throughout all of this, the 'crazy depth dwellers' observe from the vantage point of their perceptual depths. The knowledge and ocean wisdom that can be gained from these deeper strata are overlooked by the many. Some fish schools even forbid their fish from seeking these levels of strata, or condemn this older oceanic wisdom as antiquated and not relevant for the ocean of today. For this reason, most of the fish near to the surface ignore these lower depths of the ocean. They have come to the opinion that nothing of consequence can be found there; or nothing of importance can be learnt there. All the fun and excitement belong to the ocean surface. The ocean waves, the storms, the fish school competitions, the ongoing survival challenges against the predatory birds, and so on, are all there is – and it is enough to keep them occupied.

Yet the 'crazy depth dwellers' know that from time to time, fish come seeking these lower depths. And they seek assistance and knowledge about how to navigate these new strata. And how to gain perception in this deeper oceanic world. And when such fish come along, they are recognized because they have already begun to alter their fishy vibration. In fact, they need to alter their fishy vibration to truly exist at these levels. For these are the authentic vibrations of the ocean that have driven its underlying currents for time immemorial. These deep vibrations have been the heartbeat of the ocean. And if every fish listens close enough to their own heart, they will sense this vibration within them too. And if they follow this heartbeat vibration within them, they shall eventually find its resonance with the heartbeat of the Ocean Mother. This is the tale of the Ocean of Life.

The Ocean of Life is under your nose all the time. It is the very water in which you swim. Every fish secretly wishes to be aligned with the Ocean Mother. And yet, most of the fish will not perceive the subtlety of their own environment. They will not look much further than their own fish nose. Life near the surface is good enough for most fish. Why question more? It is not the fish's destiny, after all, to want to be more than a small fish drifting along near the surface of the ocean. All else are just myths and idle sea talk. Why ask about *whys* when the ocean is right before your eyes, they say.

And the fish swim on, sometimes blustered by the surface storms.

PART TWO

'A few transformed people can transform millions;
millions of untransformed people can do – or be –
next to nothing.'

Idries Shah

TWELVE

The path to a more developed resonance is not a pathway for all. First, it is necessary to understand the ways of dissonance, and how dissonance is created as part of a conditioning mechanism. This has been discussed in previous material. To arrive here, at this point, is to be at a place further along the road. Human beings often like to receive feedback – physical confirmation – to show them that they are on the right path. Synchronicity is one such feedback mechanism. And still, this remains vague for many. As you walk through the valley, we notice that you keep on shouting out, listening for your echo to return as a point of validation. Physical validation is often required, even though your physical existence is only a small range of your greater existence.

Leave to this world the things of this world. Resonate and relate with the things that vibrate to your own truth. The wounds of dislocation are now being healed across the planet, across realms, and in ways not readily visible or observed. New relations between human beings are in emergence and growth. Human beings are themselves healers when they allow the resonant energy to flow between them. The contaminant interventions are trying their best to pollute the resonant pathways. They are forcing their hand and rushing impatiently in this. Yet you – humanity – have learnt to be patient. It is not about the show but about the *BE*.

The 'vibration of being' can be communicated amongst you. You do not need to make telephone calls in order to communicate your being-resonance. The widening of the communication channels has already begun. For a long time, humanity was operating on a limited number of broadcast channels, so to speak. Yet the capacity of your vibrational wavelength has been undergoing an upgrade, and now this wavelength supports many more range of channels. More consciousness programs will be emerging into your range of vision. We could say that it is the responsibility of those persons who *can* broadcast upon these expanded range of channels, to do so. That is, to take the lead in this and become the early wave in resonant amplifiers.

Do not be dismayed by old patterns and patterning, as these shall be coming to the surface more and more as the new energies shake up the old arrangements. Some things need to be seen in order to be cleaned. Focus not on the ugliness of the dirt but on the cleaning process. In this, allow for time to move through these new arrangements. Those who crave for this old power patterning are so few. They have managed to maintain control by manipulating everything else around them. But in themselves, they are alone among humanity. We have discussed much on the Machine, which is a faceless mechanism of institutions and infrastructure. This 'faceless' aspect is being pushed more to the fore by the few for they wish to steer future directions away from human faculties. They believe that a faceless society will help create a soulless humanity. In this, the Machine will become the mother to all the little machines that shall take their places across the planet. But this scenario ignores the central element of *being-existence*. Evolvement requires life. Artificial intellect is not life – it is mechanism.

The physical body is also a tangible part of these systems within systems. It is an embedded vehicle through which the localized self can experience those aspects in physical manifested reality. For this reason, the Machine also targets the human body and its well-being for it is part of the fabric of this reality. You need to observe, sense, and be aware of your body in this respect, albeit not overly identified with it. Pursuits of physical, bodily pleasure are used to a high degree in your reality to create an over-identification and attraction to the bodily aspects. This too can, and does, lead to forms of physical addiction. If your bodily vehicle is damaged, or functions through reduced capacity, this affects your life experience. We refer here to those people who deliberately choose to mis-use and over-identify with bodily pursuits. An ailment within the body affects the nerve systems, and this affects the psychological and emotional environment also. In these times before recalibration, everything will be thrown at humanity in order to knock the collective off-balance. These are the schoolyard tricks that the few are using against the many. They are keeping you unstable through increased uncertainty and anxiety.

Much of this anxiety will be felt within the body – collectively and individually. The resonance of self affects the bodily vibration. By maintaining coherence in oneself, the body is better defended against biological instabilities. The lifeboat of humanity is being rocked at this time. The stormy waves are riding higher and shaking the boat from side to side. Yet you need to keep your navigational eye on the farther waters to which you are eventually heading. The lifeboat is not named as a 'life' boat for nothing.

You are gathering yourselves together through the storm. In this gathering, there is resonance. In your relations you shall find like-attractors and vibrational anchoring. Humanity is passing through a particular timeline, as they are referred to. Yet this wording is misleading for they are not lines, but rather as interferences, as wavelengths cross over one another and cause frequency interference. What humanity is experiencing now are these frequency interferences. Yet they are being artificially managed and manipulated to make them more disturbing than they need be. There are those amongst you who know of these larger, cosmic and planetary, dynamics. The controlling few were anticipating these moments and planned to exploit them for pushing forward their own gains and agendas.

Yet humanity has not been standing still. You are not in the disadvantage that many of you believe you are in. You are presently a little shaken – yet the vibrational realignments are coming. During these times, we suggest that those *who can*, take the responsibility to own their self – their sovereignty, reality, and truth – to be as frequency providers and vibrational beacons for others.

Establish energetic relations through self, planet, cosmos. Be in flow, but not in heavy entanglement. When you are in synch, you create more space for yourself. At this stage, what is real for you, and what is true for you, will be *for you*. This is firstly a matter for your own discernment. Truth is not something that you see. It is something that you become. And it must be true for you and your Self. And then, allow aspects of this truth to come through into your day-to-day life. Bring your experience into the mix of the physical.

You are not the 'little me' within the 'mechanism' – this is what the controlling Machine wishes you to think and feel. These are the 'whispers' that are sent around your systems. They get programmed into your societies. The whispers get amended, added to, enlarged and amplified. The whispers of 'little you' are used to formulate general obedience among the masses. It worked in the past, and the controlling few believe it will work again. Your societies are like echo chambers for these artificial whispers. These 'echo chambers' are most effective in confined spaces, whether physical or mental and emotional. Confined physical spaces are in your larger cities. Within the non-physical – what you call digital – spaces, the Machine constructs these confined echo chambers for producing mental and emotional effect amongst you. Do not overly expose yourself to these impacts. Step back.

Step back physically, mentally, emotionally, whenever it is possible to do so. The step back allows for the recalibration during this 'rest period,' as we have mentioned. The recalibration of vibration can then merge with the new synchronization.

Step Back

Rest to Recalibrate

Re-emerge to Merge

This is like a re-magnetizing of the magnet. Allowing the magnet to flow with the new current without corruption or dissonance.

Do not be put off by the show of disturbance. The new frequency will settle. Be ready for when it does. You shall find this recalibrated alignment much easier than those unprepared and already too magnetised with the old patterning.

Step back

Refresh

Re-align

THIRTEEN

It is time now to bring forth greater communication of consciousness. For what is consciousness if not an interrelated intelligence in communication? It is one and it is also present as the many. The unified state of consciousness is in constant interrelation with all the parts, yet requires relational communication. The localized aspects of consciousness are often not receiving – not picking up the phone, so to speak. Within each living cell there is the breath of consciousness. It is not a thing to be captured – it is a living, breathing presence. It is a part of the *livingness* of the cosmos. It is a life force that has been given many names within your various traditions. It has been recognized in many forms also.

The human creative expression is an aspect of consciousness being manifested. Human societies have attempted to either hide or erase knowledge of the universal nature of conscious intelligence. Many planetary rulers have hidden their power behind the outer façades of materiality. They have, and continue, to use materiality as a smokescreen. They know very well that a living conscious intelligence is the life force of existence – but they have attempted to keep this understanding from the masses. If the masses are kept in materiality, they can be kept ignorant, powerless, and constrained with these material chains. The conscious life force is then filtered and used by the few who understand its presence. But the life force cannot be contained or fenced off – it is what gives animation to all existence. Just as the words on this page cannot deny the page. You read these separate letters that form words – this is the manifestation of meaning in your 'reading reality.' Yet if you widen your perspective, you can understand that the words cannot exist without the underlying page that gives them a foundation for their existence. The many forms of human conditioning have attempted to only recognize the presence of words – and then these words are manipulated to give programmed meanings. And yet, behind the scenes, there are those of the controlling few who are attempting to harness the power of the page, the life force.

Artificial beings cannot be suddenly created into self-conscious beings. Consciousness is a vibrational sharing – a sharing of essence. All material existence emerges from this vibrational field. The cosmos, the planets, the earth, the human body – they are all degrees of vibration within the unity field. Where your state of vibration lies determines the degree of perception available to you. As in all things, the vibrational field determines the vantage point. All life is interrelated yet not all exist within the same playing field. Communication can cross over through these diverse 'playing fields.' There is communication at all times. What is needed is more listeners. How can you respond if you cannot hear the conversation?

The vantage point where you are at corresponds to your evolutionary stage. The cosmos contains a full range of these potential stages. Everything is in movement, shifting and altering vibrational possibilities. The conversation continues at all times, whether there are those willing to listen or not. Humanity has been out of the larger conversation for some time – and we can say that it is necessary for this isolation to come to a close. This communication with the life force is organic. The listener is but the speaker. The child is but the Mother. The Alpha is also the Omega. The life force is the builder, the home field of potentialities. We say that there is a 'running race' on this planet to harness this life force. The life force brings forth materiality and living expressions – and it can take it away too. What emerges can also be withdrawn, or dissolved into primal state.

What you call consciousness is a form of vibrational resonance. It is an integrative field of living intelligence. This field brings forth the potentialities for creative expressions and systems. Every physical expression emerges from conscious intelligence in energetic form. And yet, when these physical forms are cut-off from the conversation, they can be isolated and 'played with' by those who understand the grander picture. Humanity is being played with in this regard. You have been programmed not to listen. You think you are alone – amongst yourselves and amongst the cosmos – and that you live only a few short physical years. What is the meaning in this? Your life expressions then seem cruel and pointless; there is no purpose and 'anything goes.' People then run around blind within their own games and in the games of others, not knowing that all the time they are also the builder and master of the game. Without this realization, others play you and move you around the playing field.

Everything seems complex as the game rules increase. And the game appears segregated. Those controlling few have maintained their agendas and regimes of power because they have learnt how best to utilize strategies of segregation. You have segregation of nations, of peoples, of cultures and traditions, of beliefs, and of conditioning and programming. Inside each person there is a deep place of essence – a seat of conscience – that feels and knows that ALL is UNITY. And yet, the outer influences continue to push the programming of segregation, separation, and difference. The greater the system, the greater the variations of energies. There are many variations of energies within this cosmos alone. Yet the trick, so to speak, is to perceive and relate with the underlying unity that connects all. Humanity has reached a point where there is a potential now for a great leap in awareness. This awareness can lead to an opening up of the grander conversations. In this vibrational perception, the pieces will be seen as not isolated parts but as expressions of an integrated intelligence and many, many degrees of communication.

Be aware that the individual personality – or identity – will be increasingly targeted by the powers on this planet. For if the individual can be pushed further inside of their constructed identity, then they will close down their filters to the wider consciousness vibration. Identity is but a marker, a point of place, that gives a designation according to cultural norms. These human identities are now being captured to be exploited as control tags. The focus, again, is on the constriction of perception and increasingly concentrated on the material aspects. It is through these material channels that control and regulations can be applied. Consider: there is no control that can be applied over one's *essence* or *being*. The markers of control need to target the physical body, the patterns of mind, the attraction to the persona or personality, and the complete belief in one's identity. Yet, this is the external identity, a cultural construction that people invest so much of their lives in building up and protecting. People are made vulnerable when their 'identity' is attacked. It is a weak point that can be exploited, and is indeed being so.

The truth that we ask you to take responsibility for is the truth of your own *being*. In this, there is a recognition that a person's identity is their marker but it does not define who they are. People are going to be drawn more and more into these 'identity boxes' as ways to further the dislocation from greater awareness. There are cultural identities as well as biological ones. The body-mind expression is being targeted and identified and stored as *digits to define the human being*. The human DNA is being used as a 'trace identifier' and the Machine is moving fast in using this information to categorize and manage the human population. This again demonstrates the extreme in material and rational thinking. The material timeline is forcefully being actualized as the blueprint for moving forward by the controlling few upon this planet. The greater the material constriction and containment, the greater the blockage of the vibrational fields – and the greater the isolation of the human being. This is the real quarantine being put into action. The material world can be more predictable and better managed. That which is an expression of living consciousness is creative and expansive. The struggle now for humanity is to reject the increasing containment of materiality and to resonate with the living expression of the life force.

FOURTEEN

As we have stated, the vibratory life force is flowing through all living expressions, at all times. The oxygen in the air you breathe cannot be denied just because it cannot be seen. Try not breathing for several minutes. To own your truth, it is necessary to grasp that all life evolvement moves through grand cycles of change as well as smaller cycles. A lifetime of lived experience is but a short moment within an endless dance. The question that is asked of you is how you will make use of this transitory moment. The life experience is not singular. It is an integrated mix of relations and correspondences. To focus on a few separate issues is to miss the point. To be drawn into entanglement with one or two overriding issues is to live life as if through a pinpoint. It is the cultural identity that attaches to particular issues, which then can take a person down a long road of experiences. To believe in 'this thing' over all other matters, is a singular focus that has become a tight filter that blocks out many other relations with consciousness. An attachment to one particular issue should not block out the others – this is falling into the polarity trap. Be aware that different energies within a person may come forth more strongly for a time; and then step back to be replaced by other energies. Note how these waves emerge through you, but not necessarily to overly identify with them. This is a form of allowance that we spoke of in previous material.

It is important now to be aware and recognize the ever-greater array of focus points that are coming forward to grab a person's attention. These impacts and influences are coming forth now looking for bidders of their attention. The external world acts like an auction for attention. Imagine each issue to be like a cunning spirit who seeks a willing giver of attention to be attracted to them. They go in search for these attention givers. They grab onto your thread of attention and cast a spell over you. They pull you in, similar to how a fisherperson reels in a fish upon their line. People are made to believe they have found their 'truth' by attaching to a particular issue or agenda. They become a 'warrior' for this, an 'activist' for that; or a 'champion' for this cause over and above all others. The person's identity, fed upon attention, becomes fixated upon a specific issue and then adapts and molds itself around this great cause. The specificness of this type of focusing operates by excluding all those factors not within the field of concern. Filters are then built up which protect the overriding issue against the rise of all others. A person then becomes like a missile that has been programmed only to seek a particular target. This type of behaviour and energetics serves instead to limit the law of allowance.

When favoring one thing over another becomes a life mission, there is a constriction of the pathways and of potentialities. We speak of this because 'one's truth' can easily become a fixation rather than a realization of allowance. Any idea, issue, thought pattern, belief, or behavior that blocks the pathway towards perception of truths can be considered as a disease. It is a dis-ease for it takes a person out of synch and out of balance from their natural ease. To begin with, a person must recognize the ailment and perceive the symptoms:

Someone asked a wise man, 'I have heard that humanity is suffering from an ailment which prevents men and women from seeing truth, from knowing themselves. What is the main symptom?'

The wise man answered:

'The first symptom is to believe that one is *not* suffering from this illness at all. But when it *really* starts to take hold, the patient may *agree* that he is ill, but now insists that the disease is anything other than actually it is.'

It can be recognized here why so much of our earlier communications were based around the theme of human conditioning. Without the realization and understanding of the predicament, a person does not believe there is a problem. Least of all, do they grasp that there is great disease operating through their reality perception.

If everyone is standing on their heads, how do you convince someone that they are seeing the world upside-down?

FIFTEEN

We have touched upon the subject of human identity as a social and cultural construct. To take this a step further, we ask you to consider the identity of the human being *as a human*. The further evolvement of the human race is anticipated and expected. There are further pathways to travel, and new potentialities to emerge. There are faculties inherent within the human body that have not yet emerged within the collective species. There have been advanced individuals living amongst humanity in each epoch, as is generally the case. Just as some flowers bloom first, so too are there sensitive individuals within the collective that display early signs of new abilities and capacities. The biological human body is a living organism in partnership with the life force of the cosmos. Each cell of the human body has vibrational qualities and is in communication with other vibrational fields. Throughout the human body, there is a conscious intelligence.

What we put forth here is that a 'living identity' is an intelligence in correspondence with other vibrational fields. To be 'fully human' is to be a *more evolved human*. Now consider the advancement in synthetic technologies upon the planet, and the organizations managing this research. There is a difference between an 'enhanced human' and an 'evolved human.' One is natural and organic, and the other is synthetic. There is a problematic pathway emerging in your reality that concerns the use of certain advanced technologies to interfere with the vibratory signature of the organic human being. As we have said, the human being is a receptor, processor, and transmitter of the consciousness frequency. The human is a part of the whole communication web of intelligence. The more evolved human being integrates further into this resonance of intelligence. Evolvement is always in a direction toward unification with Source, and not away from it. If there is lack of unity understanding within the human race, as we observe there is, then this is not the time to be advancing integration with synthetic technologies. Humanity needs to come from a place of greater unity within itself. Otherwise, the potential for greater segregation exists.

The push for mergence of human being with synthetic technologies is primarily for outer gratification and enhanced abilities. This is an extreme display of material thinking. The integration that results from this is not an organic one but an integration of information and material data. We see here another pathway for the intervention of external control measures into the life of the human being. You must observe from where these declarations are being made and what agendas they favor. In this time, we do not see these agendas as being in your favor. On the contrary, they are emerging from the systems of the Machine. This controlling power structure considers the human race as parts within its own machinic arrangement. To think in parts is a lower expression of consciousness.

To own your truth is to not allow others to take you away from yourself. This is the splintering, the process of fragmentation. There is more to come still yet from humanity. There are those who wish to attempt to change the conversation. They say – 'humanity has come to the end of its natural growth. To survive, it must adapt and merge with machines.' This is not a living conversation but one that is rooted within a limited material perception. It is also a planned viewpoint that is being utilized to further the agenda of control over humanity. It is being used with full knowledge that this is not a pathway that is yet ready to benefit the future growth of the human species.

The human species has an innate, in-built capacity for its further evolvement. This evolvement is not a separate pathway but is entwined with many layers of energies and vibrational fields that connect species with planet and cosmos. To consider humanity as a separate object apart from its environmental and universal surroundings is short of sight and dangerously misaligned. Life is transactional. The energies and flows of life are reciprocal. To fully interact and participate, one should do so from their own state of being – from one's *own truth*. This is the greatest foundation possible for enabling communication and cognitive awareness of expansive intelligence. Do not seek outside of yourself for material solutions to the question of how to become a fully human being. The necessary growth is from inside to out. It is not a solution to add a synthetic part to you and claim this as a 'greater you.'

The individual will be facing this question of their identity in the coming years. Each species and race of beings have had to arrive at a collective understanding of their identity as expressions of Source. The path to this arrival comes through the experiences of each individual currently within a life experience. There is no way to avoid coming to terms with one's Self. It is like trying to run away from your feet.

The more a person looks outside of themselves for a solution, the more will grow their exterior reality with things that will look like solutions. The external world will mirror the wants of the individual. This is a tricky maze, for it can entice a person further and further out of themselves and attaches their vibration to external frequencies of the physical world. The external world, like the reflective pond, wants for you to look at it – to admire it and fall into attraction with it. The more you do so, the harder it becomes to pull yourself away from this reflection.

We are not saying that the external world should not be enjoyed. This would not be correct. There are great wonders, delights, awe, and positive happenings to be experienced and learnt from. There is much joy in the immersion with physical life. It is when enjoyment turns to an unbalanced consumption that an imbalance emerges. And, as we say, these outer attachments then grow as if to fulfil a desire from yourselves. This is part of the reciprocal nature of interaction with vibrational fields.

When a balance is tipped, it needs to be restored. This restoration has been overdue for humanity and the imbalance has become substantial. The greater the degree of tipping, the grander is the movement required to return to balance. The dissonance of this is clearly being felt in your dimension now. So many factors have been taking humanity off-track, both natural diversions and deliberate distractions. What was once useful at one time to guide you back to the path may no longer be a useful guide.

When some teachings were meaningful at a particular point in your pathway, if they are prolonged, and tainted with human necessities and gratifications, their purpose becomes detrimental. The past has brought you to where you now find yourself. To move ahead, begin with knowing what you know in this very moment.

The old gods were part of an older story.

The human potential is there to be nurtured, for it was always there and never not present. The outer truths were as crutches for you to learn how to walk by your own aid – by your *own truth*.

SIXTEEN

We would like to return here to the subject of intentionality. We have mentioned before the importance of this theme – the act of deliberate, conscious focus and projection. For many people, it is as if consciousness passes them by, like a breeze that only gently touches them and makes them aware of its presence. In this sense, consciousness is taken for granted. It is something that just 'is' – that happens to exist from complex brains, and humans are lucky enough to have it coming from their brains. This is the standard model of thinking, which itself shows a lower form of conscious intelligence. This is what we observe to be the 'passive mode' of consciousness. It is not reached for, grasped for, but just used when a minimal amount of thinking and communication is required. For the rest of the time, it remains like unused water in the bathtub. This is such lazy thinking.

Consciousness is a creative, dynamic, and intelligent field. It is immersive; that is, it is responsive. As we have previously noted, your quantum physics has gained some of this insight to the extent that some scientists now refer to your reality as 'participatory.' Consider this: consciousness is something that is to be participated with, not passively left alone. And participation requires intent; knowing and aware participation requires deliberate, conscious intent. As in all things, there are degrees – and participation also responds in degrees according to depth, cognition, and awareness. The less conscious intent the individual has now, the less involved they will be in the shifts that are to come. And the more they will be at the whim of the storms that rock the surface waves.

It is necessary to grasp that human consciousness is responsive to the discipline and focus in which you engage with it. And similarly, so does your reality respond to engagement. This is the nature of the Game, so to speak. It is an immersive and responsive environment within which a life experience is acquired. In this environment, you are the swimmers. Why sit on the shore, waiting for someone to come along and show you how to swim? You already know how to swim. Yet there are many who prefer to stay on the shore – to sit back, relax, and 'get a tan.' These are the same people who play the 'pity me' card and then expect to be provided a boat free of cost. We are not being critical here. We only wish to show how this appears under observation. Those people that understand this are those that know better and should not allow themselves to slip back into this behavior. For those that do not yet understand, they still have time and opportunities to learn. Some of them will learn from observing those who know, and who act. All creatures learn from observation and mimicry to some degree. After that, they have to push themselves forward on their own intent and energy.

Do not sell yourselves short. You can all be equal players. The gameboard is not equal because it has been tampered with. Yet your portion of the gameboard can be according to your own participation if you are cautious not to easily slip into the gaming area of others. Your own truth is not to play the victim for others. It is to not be disenfranchised from what you truly are. Some of you may feel excluded from the society or culture around you. This is due to a difference now in your resonance. Take this as a positive sign – a sign of discernment. But do not take this to mean an exclusion or an alienation from one's self. There is no true alienation from the Self. In this, it is important to separate self from society – they both require different forms of nourishment. An unhelpful vibrational loop can sometimes manifest when self and society are trying to share the same vibrational patterns. Know your own patterns, your own resonance, and come forward from this place. Do not throw off your vibrational overcoat just because someone in the society tells you so – do not turn yourself inside out to become what you are not.

Intention is also about holding one's vibrational patterns in place. Things will fall into relation according to where you place yourself. In trying to fall in line with every shift and movement in your external environments, it is like the child chasing the shadows of the clouds across the playing field. This chasing takes the child in all directions, and yet they are but tricks of light. In owning your truth, you are the clouds, and you have the intent to choose how to cast your shadows from the light upon the grassy playing field. You are not running around, here and there – you have the focus of how, when, and where to participate.

If an individual is fractured and imbalanced within, then their intent will lose focus and directionality. It will also lack vibratory coherence. We are not saying that you should be walking through life in intense states of concentration. This is only likely to give you more headaches. What we say is: gather yourself, balance, and focus with conscious awareness. This can be done lightly. Intention and focus do not need to be heavy. Indeed, is the light of the sun heavy? Is the concentration of love, heavy?

It is time to be direct with yourselves. Indirectness is not being truthful within. Why place a space between who you think you are, and who you know yourself to be? Start to live more through the truth of who you know yourself to be. Put this into your actions and interactions. Project this into the participatory nature of your reality. If you continue to play at being someone else, reality will come to recognize you as this other person – and will respond to this 'other you' accordingly. Let reality know who you really are, and then see what comes up for you.

Human consciousness allows humanity to be sentient in physical expression – to have cognition, to think and feel, and to consider these thoughts and feelings. Yet it too has a purpose beyond this. Human consciousness is a resonance for the planet also. Every resonance is a resonance for multiple fields. In this, a focused consciousness (intention) is not only supporting you but has other purposes within your reality. When a human being genuinely and truly serves themselves, but not in selfish greed but in evolvement, then they also serve the evolvement beyond them. All things are wheels within wheels, as you say.

The human vibration is a receiver. In this, it allows flow and transmission for other purposes. When you block this, you also block it for other needs. Consider the state of many human beings upon this planet, and then consider the state of the planet. All is intertwined. Humanity shares with the heartbeat of the planet. All outer beats synch up with the inner heart beats.

SEVENTEEN

There are a great deal of reflections and illusions being played out and utilized within your reality and across your physical realms. Humanity has spent a long time staring into the reflections and so little time in individual reflection upon this. There is a great difference here. To stare into and be distracted and consumed by the reflections pulls the attention outwards. Again, we feel it necessary to return to the subject of attention. The awareness of one's attention, and the attention upon one's awareness are critical now.

If you consider all the distractions and 'pretty reflections' that have existed, and been provided for you by your societies, you will see that they exist to take the human attention away from itself. To be more precise, it is to take away from the individual the power of conscious attention. This then is transformed into a form of automatic, or robotic, attention. Through this robotic, mechanical attention, much of humanity has learned to exist and to 'make the best of their lives.' It is a form of living through the mechanical mode. This mode has its uses, in particular areas. When the mechanical aspects are functioning well, this allows the creative and conscious energies to be put into active use. You are not aware of your digestion, are you? Most people are even not aware of their heart beating, or of their breathing. These are automatic functions that can operate outside of conscious participation. This is also the same when the body-mind has learnt certain tasks – this can be such as riding a bike, washing the floor, brushing the teeth. Such tasks as these are viewed as robotic in general (when not in extreme). Once learnt, the conscious mind allows these tasks to be run 'in the background' by the mechanical aspects. This has served the human being well when these processes are in harmony with each other. Yet, we observe that your societies have long been covertly programming and developing the mechanical-robotic side of the human being.

Observe this in your cultural programs: in your education, entertainment, jobs, responsibilities, and more. The impacts provided have been increasingly developed to target and make dominant the mechanical aspect of the human. As the individual learns, and becomes comfortable, with the dominance of their mechanical, automated side, so does this also corrupt the capacity of conscious attention. What we mean here is that *attention dulls*. The power of concentrated, conscious attention is less required in your societies. There is less demand for this type of functioning. Like a muscle, the less it is used or required, the more it weakens through lack of use. The power of attention is diluted, and then slips into automatic mode. This automatic mode of attention has long been the aim of much of your media. Attention has been made passive through your television and visuals. Also, through much of your entertainment. More recently, entertainment has become increasingly visually powerful and dynamic. The more dynamic it becomes, the more that human attention is required to 'sit back' and just 'observe the show.' It is a sort of bombardment of your senses. And more senses overload only but increases the state of 'attention passivity.' If you observe this in your societies and in the cultural impacts, you will recognize this increased stimulus to make passive the human attention. Often, it is a form of *mesmerisation*. We suggest you research the origins of 'Mesmer' and discover its relation to hypnotism.

The reflections in your outer world are mesmerizing, hypnotic, and trance-like. This is deliberate, and they are the plays of the Machine, for they serve to increase the automated, robotic side of the human being. The more this programming is increased and processed by you, the more it becomes integrated into your body-mind. That is, the more it will re-wire your own pathways. This is the contrary path against human evolvement. Contrary to evolvement through rewiring your thinking patterns and perceptions so that the human body-mind can receive and transmit a different vibrational set or wavelength.

If the human being becomes increasingly automated and robotic, where is the free will? This is a big topic amongst humans – free will. Many of you believe that you possess it, and that it is a natural, born 'given.' In your out-dated philosophy you declare: *I think, therefore I am.* The robot-human thinks – therefore it IS? You see the confusion in this?

Genuine free will does not operate through the mechanical aspects of humankind. It can only be exercised through conscious awareness of your experience within your life expression.

Instead of being drawn into the reflections of your world and being consumed by them, you can consciously reflect your Self into your reality program. That is, be the producer – be the driver of your actions. This is the expression of your <u>will</u>. To have a will of your own, you need to consciously participate and interact within life. Free will is an expression of your conscious alignment, balance, and synchronization with the shifting frequencies in your reality. As the frequencies 'evolve,' or shift, so too does humanity, if it is operating through free will rather than constraint and confinement. And to participate in this evolvement consciously and with awareness is now the remit and responsibility of humanity.

Free will is to align with all that you are. To exhibit free will is to also *own your truth.*

The mechanical side of humanity is that part which dances among the shadows and allows disillusioned minds to become entangled in their collective reflections and shimmering waters. This is why we come back to focus on the theme of human attention. Your attention is being taken away from you, and many of you give it away willingly. You are being entertained into mechanicalness. Much of humanity is being amused into the passive state. It is a state of *attention inebriation.* You are being taken out of your attention and into a state of senseless intoxication. This can be through physical substances such as narcotic elements and alcohol. It is also increasingly through entertaining distractions and forms of approved leisure. These are your comforts. These are all strategies to inoculate as many people as possible into the robotic side of life. When in this passive state, increased perceptions and cognition are very difficult. Mostly, the people who live their lives in the mechanical state have no will, desire, or need for increasing their perceptual and cognitive faculties. They remain in the low vibrational state. Their resonance, in this state, is vibrational food for the Machine. That is why we say that conscious attention and awareness are important. Own them too, for they shall bring you to your own truths.

EIGHTEEN

There continues to be much talk on 'doomsday' scenarios and the end of the human species. Some people consider that humanity is in a 'make or break' time and that there is great possibility that human beings could soon cease as a race. We do not consider this as a correct analysis. We observe that such commentaries fall into the mythos, long present within human history, to see all great cyclic shifts as apocalyptic or extinction-level events. The 'end of the world' has always been a common theme amongst many of your historical myths. The great difference at this moment – and this is an important one – is that you now are living through this time.

All existence is a continuation. There are many elements in each life expression that are unique to that particular 'life reality.' Many life expressions contain their particular 'good' and 'evil' aspects. What is present in one reality may not exist or be relevant within another. Evolvement takes many forms and many paths, and is intertwined with various environmental and cosmic factors. There is an incredible range and scale of adaptability and creativity within material life realities. You do not know what is going to happen to you for there are many particulars and specifics that have not yet been decided, chosen, or actualized. There is no 'End' – there are transformations. Such transformations occur in both vibrational and energetic form, as well as in physical-material form.

What we do put forth here is that there are unwelcome elements in your current reality that are trying to push for an extreme path from a place of instability and incoherent vibration. Such attempts will only amount to further imbalances within your reality systems. It is like asking an inexperienced person to pilot a plane with hundreds of passengers on-board who place their trust in this pilot. Similarly, there are forces attempting now to pilot Plane Humanity, and they lack the correct intentions, motivations, and alignments. In this scenario, we have suggested that the passengers take back the plane for themselves and disallow the pilot from being in the cockpit. We say: do not attack with weapons. Instead, recalibrate the vibration of the plane so that the pilots, and others like them, will not find it possible to be on board for it is no longer comfortable or a part of their reality.

You see now that reality is an interactive mix, and the values are what you have collectively agreed upon to represent the gameplay for your particular reality. As in all games, there are those who wish to cheat and 'bend the rules' or ignore them completely. The first reaction is often one of 'outcry' – uproar and protest. But you see how these protests only serve to focus the attention onto the injustice and enhancing the predicament. The game then starts to become attracted around where these attentions are placed, and pathways are then established around the injustice and uproar. What we say is that this is not the most efficient use of energies. These energies are being directed into this 'problem spot' in your life game rather than being redirected or transferred into creating alternative vibrational alignments and placing the attention onto other, more beneficial pathways. Too much 'attention-energy' is, we say, being used up in projecting onto the 'good' and 'bad' polarity in your reality and can be served better as creative energies for evolvement beyond the confines of your value judgements. This is an observation – not a criticism.

The distractions used to restrict your attention, and constrict your consciousness, are not always in the nature of grand events. They are subtle also. Anything that takes you away from yourself is a strategy of increasing the automation in you. Some of these strategies include using your own value sets against you. See: you arrive in this reality and wish to know the game rules. You are taught the main rules, and then are programmed with many extra side-rules that apply according to the location (culture/society) in which is your immersive environment. On top of these you are told what values are necessary to be upheld, and then these values are then diversified over time to include a whole range of sub-values according to one's opinion system. And yet, instead of you playing by these rules – they are exploited to *play you*. You are manipulated into reactions, emotional responses, mental states, and more, by certain forces tweaking these game rules (values, ethics, opinions, beliefs, morals) and distorting these to 'push and shove' the masses in predicted directions. As we have said: do not think that those who try to control you have not studied this Game, and how to manipulate this reality. They have studied humanity too – for a very long time. They can predict how the automated human will react. They can make accurate predictions on how to steer the mechanical masses. Yet they are unable to know or predict how the genuine, creative human being – the individual who *owns their truth* – will respond and act. The *true you* is their blind spot. And they know this. That is why they try to bring all the people out of their blind spot and into the light of exposure.

The conditioning of certain stories and myths is one way to bring people out of their authenticity and into the main net of mechanical behavior. Certain directions are always herded as the main one. Those who go against the direction of the herd often find themselves receiving social stress, ridicule, and a great pressure to conform. The pressure to conform is a herd instinct – a collective social belonging - which has been utilized much over human history. This is because it requires less resources from the few in the hierarchy of control. The masses from the lower end of the social pyramid of power are used as the enforcers of pressure and conformity. Some of this we explained in previous material ('Own Your Sovereignty'). Those individuals whose only truth is external to them will be more receptive to peer pressure. They are weaker and less resistant to social pressure for they have no center of truth, no foundation of selfhood, within them. They are external creatures, dependent upon the opinions and beliefs of others to sustain them.

What we say is that the person who has come to *own their truth* has established their own form of sustenance. They participate and contribute to their society (or not) through conscious choice and not through the pressure of conformity. They have their <u>will</u> and their <u>freedom</u> to act or not to act. By freedom, we do not mean freedom of mobility, for physical containment may still occur. What we refer to is a state of freedom within. An individual can be physically incarcerated for their lifetime, yet if they have freedom within then they will always be a free person. Another person can have a life of liberty and movement, and all the attractions of the world - yet if they do not have freedom within, then they shall never be truly free.

Each person carries their freedom or their imprisonment with them wherever they go.

NINETEEN

The many truths within your reality are like stories. They change over time; they are misinterpreted and can carry treasure as well as misconceptions. Any story that is passed between many people gets amended, adapted, and added to. It is like the story of whispers: it starts as one thing and ends up at the final listener as something different. Sometimes the 'truth,' as it has been told, is said to be beyond you – in a realm beyond that of humanity. Yet this is a mis-truth, for each one of you carries the seed within that can make the connection to your greater truth.

When the important things are placed outside of you – your gods and your creators – then there is a space for others to manipulate this intermediate connection. What is placed outside of yourselves makes you vulnerable, for there is a space of dependency. When it is within you, there is nothing to come between 'it' and you. This is why for so long within human societies and their artificial hierarchies, they have given stories about the truths being beyond you. In this, there was a deliberate intention to take the majority of human beings away from themselves. A 'governing factor' was placed over humanity from its earliest beginnings. Humanity's eyes looked up to the skies for the answers. Benedictions and requests were given to the creators in the high heavens above you. All this represented yet more systems within systems, creating yet more hierarchies. When there are such systems and hierarchies, it is easy for those few who wish to control the many to enter into these levels and manipulate them. Such systems could then be more easily reflected onto your societies to establish yet more hierarchical structures as physical realities. Humanity's early questioning soon became crystalized into solid, social systems which became external forms of governance and structures for control. Everything began from taking the imaginings within and projecting them onto structures without that could be governed. This is the pattern that has continued until this time.

The evolvement now needed within humanity cannot be accomplished by continuing to put things outside of yourselves. This more primitive pattern of thinking and behavior has reached its point of end validity. It has, as you say, reached its 'sell-by-date.' To move forward now in growth and evolvement, humanity must bring itself back within.

The emphasis you are currently placing outside of yourselves is on a world that is broken and needs to be fixed. This is more of the externalizations. Yet if humanity remains divided within itself – divided collectively and individually – then no true healing (what you call 'fixing') can take place. You would not go to a schizophrenic doctor to ask advice, for you would not be sure if what the doctor said one day would be the same as the next. The healing – the doctor's advice – must come from a place of unity, balance, and perceptive understanding that is not corrupted. There are players on your planet that are pushing their agendas by creating certain 'truth stories' about the world. It is easy to get pulled into and persuaded by these stories so that they become *your* stories and *your* truths. This has always been the most effective trick to maintain management over people. The trick is to get people to believe that it is 'their truths' that they are representing. In many cases, humans have been unknowingly programmed with mis-truths. Once a mis-truth has been assimilated and adopted by a person or group, it is very difficult to undo this programming. People cling on to their truths more than most any other thing.

This is why we say it is most important that a person learn to distinguish, and to discern, what is true for them, genuinely and sincerely, and then to learn how to *own their truth*. These are not just some pleasant-sounding words we are using in these communications. We are wishing for each individual to understand their patterns of thinking and behavior, and to learn how to distinguish what is true and right for them. Reality itself consists of different ordering of patterns. These patterns form energetic frequencies. Frequency-sets are what establish manifestations in your reality. In order to move forward, it is necessary to understand the foundation of your reality. For if you do not understand amongst yourselves, then there will always be the very few who place themselves 'at the top' who will use this knowledge to benefit themselves.

The majority of thought patterns place the truths and meanings of life outside of you. This is the eternal external chasing – as the cat chases its shadow and ignores the sun.

We are not saying that the past patterns and structures have been detrimental. Many were appropriate for their time – and some even necessary. It was necessary to have enough focus and involvement with physical structures for humanity to develop its civilizations and material needs. A great material phase was required to create the necessary structures that now provide you with the comfort of living most people experience. Yet this phase also contained its own imbalances that allowed for greed and control to infiltrate. We say now: bring yourself to the present so that the future can be understood. If the way forward is manifested from the present state of imbalance, extreme polarities, and controlling mechanisms, then the future will be formed upon those patterns and energetic frequencies. To step without, it is now paramount for you to step within. The Machine would be happy to have many of you worried, with anxiety, and running around the world shouting out for everybody to 'fix the world.' And then there are more shouting and negotiating about how to do, who to do, what to do. And then, who is on what side and who is not. Then the games begin as usual, with sides taken and the 'us vs. them' polarities. It is the same patterns – only the subject has changed. If it is not your gods that humanity is fighting over, then it is their lands. Then it is their oceans. Now it is the air and the winds. Anything can be fit into this patterning. This is all fuel to feed the same engine – the engine of the Machine.

All this may seem laudable – yet we say again, it takes you away from yourselves. Why fight a cause when you yourself are the cause and the needed focus of attention? The mis-truths of your stories say that this needs to be straightened out and fixed. What they do not include in these stories is the recalibration and re-aligning of pathways within and between human beings. It is not a 'fixing' that is required now but a *realignment*. This realignment is vibrational and will assist in bringing forth a resonance for this reality experience.

Adapting to physical life and its externality was indeed necessary. Yet over time it came also to signify a loss of contact with Self, and a form of individualism that was limited to the superficial personality. The internal contact with Self/Source was diminished as attention became drawn further into the externals. The conversation that humanity used to have with the higher realities became shut down over time. It was kept alive by the few. Yet for the majority of humanity, they went into exile. This state of exile has been maintained and sustained by a range of 'controlling powers' who wish to keep humanity incommunicado with itself. Pathways for finer perception and more expansive cognition were shut down also and sealed into restrictive boxes of reality programming. The domain of the *seen* overtook the realm of the *unseen*. It is far easier for a seeing person to be made blind than it is for a blind person to be made to see.

We wish for humanity to see now.

Yet first, you need to see yourselves.

This is the inside-outness of your current situation. Human beings must come to see that they have been blinded and to learn to see again from within this perceptive blindness. What did once serve its purpose is no longer doing so. It is fine and good to move on now. It is time to move house and give thanks to the place of your previous lodging. Your family needs have expanded – neither the house nor its location now serves your requirements. Allow things to fall away. Allow so many of the mis-truths you are hearing to fall away. Re-pattern your thinking so that new internal pathways can be established that are aligned with the new broadcast. It is a broadcast that you now need to hear – it is speaking about your evolvement.

TWENTY

There is no genuine truth in suffering. We say this for we observe now that types of physical suffering continue to be advanced upon the planet. Almost all human societies are orientated for conflict. Social constructs are biased and often based on the premise of the suffering of others. There is now also an increase in the domestic suffering of people within what you call your advanced societies. The outward gaze of attention has reached its limit. Intention without inner awareness only gives birth to mechanical processes. Observe the stories and 'social truths' now rampant in your societies. Do they come from a place of inner realization – or do they come from a mechanical place? The heart of humanity will continue to suffer if the outward gaze does not align with your inner truths.

The potentials for evolvement are those that are to come from within the true sense of the human being. Physical structures and 'thinking objects' cannot lead the way ahead. Humanity is evolving to gain its own direct experience and communication with the life force. There is no need for this potential for direct experience to be delayed longer. It is time to move out of the bubbles or filters of distortion. It is time to gather momentum. There are always the many that remain within distortion and within the conditioning of the main programs of the Machine. You cannot force change onto those who are not yet willing to make change within themselves. Again, do not put your attention onto the struggle with others. Instead, participate with the new momentum now gathering. There will be increasing temptations to be fixated on others, on the actions and beliefs of others, and a desire to rush in to 're-educate' and 'save' them. Yet when you are out there trying to convert others, your energy is not available for the vibratory momentum now required. People have their ideals that drive them. Yet each person must make the personal journey from their ideals to their self-realization.

Ideals are far from realizations. Ideals are often what restrict you – realizations are what can set you free from this. Humans have the capability to turn things around. Not 'super' humans but ordinary humans; yet in truth, no human is just ordinary.

Self-aware consciousness carries its own potential for power and manifestation. It is important to distinguish between 'their story' and 'their truths' and *your story* and *your truths*. This is a question of your own inner authority. If you observe with external attention, you will be swamped with information/propaganda from their side. And things will seem overwhelming. It is necessary to make the observations from a space within – a place of rest and quiet. This is the rest period we have spoken about. Then you shall not be swayed by the programming of mis-truths. Conscious awareness is about focusing the creative impulse with intent. A dull form of awareness is more swayed and influenced by the visual, the spectacle, the dynamic and that of heightened emotion. It is these forms of the visual and the spectacles that have begun to increase their manipulation of truths. This is being accelerated through your channels of technology, and the digital forms. They can play with these 'truth stories' and present them in many various styles. So many methods, adapted to different societies and cultures, that the inconsistency only confuses and leads to increased susceptibility amongst many of you. You shall not find your truths amidst this jungle. The pathways of the multitudinous 'truth-jungles' are deliberately meant to mislead and misdirect. Those that walk there without an inner anchor become lost – and ultimately lost to themselves.

It has become more noticeable now that the lines have been drawn. For those with eyes to see, it is clear who and what aligns itself with which particular resonance. We feel now there is no excuse in discernment. For those that cannot see, or have not seen until now, they may never perceive what is now before you. Humanity has arrived at a point where many choices have now been made. Those with inner authority have made, or begin to make, the choices that are necessary for them. These decisions, and the ability to make them from a place of inner authority, create a resonance that then becomes your mirror world – your mirror resonance. This reflection also strengthens resonance, which then allows for more inner pathways to open up; then these inner pathways establish outer pathways, and your reality becomes affected by this form of participation.

Human evolvement is a vibrational 'mix' and 'match' of resonances. A refinement of vibrations also allows for evolution to occur within physical bodies – human bodies as well as planetary bodies. All physical 'bodies' are vibrational constructs. As physical bodies change and adapt, so then do they change their vibrational frequency and their resonance fields. All is recurring back into itself and affecting all movement and change. All is interrelating with itself. You can say that this is the 'dance of life.' It is hard to define these processes as one thing or another. They are not isolated or separate processes. Know this, for it shall assist you in your relational understanding and energetic relations. Your truth is that you are at play within this flux and flow of consciousness. It is your perceptual prison – your confinement of consciousness – that attempts to shut you out and place you, humanity, in self-confinement.

When you think it is about one thing or another – about 'this' but not 'that' – then you are being blinded by the false light. You are mesmerized by the light of the bulb in your small room, yet do not look beyond to see the immensity of the sun.

To become aligned with your own truth, you may first need to accept the discomfort that you feel in not knowing. This discomfort represents the uncertainty when first letting go of external dependencies to gain your freedom of thought and consciousness. It is like when as a child you first learned to ride a bicycle. A parent or guardian figure – an adult – would first be holding the bike to keep it stable whilst you, as the child, learned how to peddle. You then learned to peddle the bike, yet you had not learned how to be stable by yourself. At some point, the supervising adult has to let go. Maybe at first you wobble and then fall off your bicycle. Perhaps you scratch your knees. It's okay – isn't it? You get back on the bicycle and try again. Another wobble. Another fall. Eventually, with enough attempts, you finally manage to stabilize the bicycle yourself. And how do you feel? You feel euphoric – you feel wondrous. You made it.

You gained one of your earliest freedoms. After that, you don't wish to go inside your home. You spend all day outside on your bicycle. Your parents shout for you. But you don't wish to come inside yet – you are loving your newfound freedom.

Imagine this scenario a million or more times greater?

From the discomfort, the wobble, and the fall, comes well-deserved freedom. You have earned it. And you come to realize that it was within you all long. It was never not there – you only had to train yourself to release it during your 'physical childhood.' Learning to ride was one of your learning experiences on the path to adulthood.

Humanity is upon a similar path to its cosmic adulthood. There is so much more to learn, experience, and express. At the heart of this is vibration and conscious intelligence. At various points along the way, you need to drop your supporting structures, just as you took away the stabilizers from the bicycle. You need to pass beyond each of these similar points in order to reach toward your own maturity. You will not find yourselves in any outer structures. Your own truths will not be found in any of these external forms or 'stabilizers.' In the end, it all has to come back to you. For in truth, there is no 'spirituality' out there. There are games, toys, rituals, and reflections. There is no word or words that you need. You are *exactly where you are.*

Don't try to name it as one thing or the other. There is no need to try to fill your inner space with new popular structures of the day. If you do this, it is like the animal that stands on the hot desert sands, moving from one foot and then to the other, then back to the other, to avoid too much heat. And yet, the animal stays still. Lift your feet off the hot sands of materiality.

Fly according to your own truths, for they shall navigate you when there is no land at your feet and no maps. For you shall be your own guidance. It is time now.

TWENTY ONE

The reality trying to gain dominance upon this planet is seeking agreement from humanity. The human tendency to not disagree with this dominance creates an allowance for it to manifest. Humanity is not a single pattern – a single wavelength. Every manifestation seeks its own expansion of the consciousness experience. When a few, a minority, then get into a position to develop a pathway that blocks this expansion for others, then it becomes an aberrant vibration within the overall creative flow. Such an aberrant vibratory pathway is more like a 'glitch in the system.' It has no long-term positive longevity. Positive, creative conscious expression is a powerful force. To attempt to divert the natural flow and expansion of this force is a hazardous endeavor. It is unpredictable and creates a great deal of disharmony and imbalance. These are the wobbles now being experienced. Humanity has not yet learned to stabilize its own ride toward adulthood and maturity. Yet these decisions are now at hand.

Consciousness is an amazingly powerful force. It does not become subdued easily. The greatest strategy against you is one of amnesia. Many physical expressions of consciousness are unaware, are ignorant, of their true nature and potential. The razzle dazzle of your mirror world distracts the majority. The sleeping masses enjoy their trance willingly. This is a huge 'sleeping pressure' to keep under control. Those of you awake enough to know of this great scheme against you, and against your evolvement, must now align with your own truths. Inner authority can become an intention to be focused with understanding and alignment. Your own truths are your path to freedom. For this reason, we say to you: *Own Your Truth.*

> *'Then you will know the truth,*
> *and the truth will set you free.'*
>
> (JOHN, 8:32)

It seems the period of disruption is now upon you. This, as we have said, is part of the experience of your 'learning wobble.' This is a vibrational pattern that needs to be stabilized in time. Too much wobble, and another 'fall off the bicycle' occurs, and another bruising of the knees, so to speak. Humanity has fallen off the bicycle several times already. Every time you get back on to the bicycle, a great deal of time is needed to rebuild your civilization as you start over once again. Humanity needs to stabilize its ride into adulthood before the winter arrives. Winter storms disrupt a great deal the art of bicycle riding. Your learning needs to be achieved during the 'summer months.' A new pattern of stabilization is now required in order to be prepared for the pathways ahead.

We sense that there will be a certain number of human beings that will not be around for this learning process to be accomplished. There will be some further shifts and 'comings and goings' amongst you. Do not lose focus during these movements. Choose your vibrational path and align with it.

When you are closer to your truths, you will understand that there is no need to lose energy confronting the rights and wrongs of others and their opinions. Each intention is each individual's energetic allowance. The focus now is not to become lost in the ego expressions of others, but to align with the forces and flows of like-resonance. As we brought forth in our previous material, it is necessary to represent the law of allowance. It is this understanding that shall assist in aligning with relational frequencies. The focus can be upon human betterment and evolvement through gaining inner authority and by owning one's sovereignty, reality, and truth.

Be assured and calm in facing humanity's critical times.

Be in remembrance.

Be with intention.

In the face of external uncertainties and injustices, it is easy to fall away from one's intention. It should be kept in remembrance that for any new frequency patterns to be manifested through physical reality, a good deal of focused

155

intention is required. It is a time to recognize that individual stability and balance is of utmost importance. There will be much learning to experience the new human adventure, and it may not all be roses, as you say.

Personal agendas are not the same as individual truths. It is the moment now for the human being to detract itself from the entanglement and energies of personal agendas and vendettas, and to align with universal betterment. There are alignments with the collective need as well as individual truths. There need not be any conflict between these for they always should be in balance for correct species evolvement. Expanded consciousness for the individual is of benefit to the collective for they are relational.

Re-patterning vibrational pathways will mean that new value structures will come into being. Certain cultural and localized value systems will need to be replaced by values that are more in alliance with the growth needs of the present, for the future. In this, allow for some things to unfold before other, new arrangements can emerge. It may be uncomfortable for a time during this wobble, yet allow this also as stimulus for focusing one's individual self and priorities. Allow the disruptive wobble period to re-align yourself. This is an opportunity also for the expansion of truth-consciousness and its manifestation within physical reality.

As we have said from the beginning of our communications, everything is related to consciousness – from its restriction (tyranny) to its expansion (freedom). All is an expression of consciousness. It is important to shift away from an expression of victim consciousness (low vibration) into creative consciousness. Creative consciousness can be expressed in both the active and non-active states. That is, from conscious participation to observer mode – according to the localized necessities of the time, the place, and the people – and, above all, one's individual, appropriate state of being.

Each individual may sense a strong pull to certain objectives they feel are necessary to be accomplished. This is each individual's Path and can only be decided upon by one's self. Each person is to consider what their contribution may be. Again, it need not be an active one. It can also come from the contribution of one's state of being and resonance. Deep within all human awareness is the knowing – the intuitive understanding – that humankind is here to achieve its evolvement. Just as there are individual objectives, so there are evolutionary ones. The potential for humanity's greater intelligence to be made manifest and to participate within the expansive cosmos amongst other intelligent races remains strong. There are also other forces not aligned with this greater potential. And yet, consciousness always, but always, pushes towards its greater expression and knowing. Consciousness wishes to be known – and to know itself.

Your unique life experience is in your hands now. This is about your truth, your knowing, your apprehension, understanding, and awareness. It is upon you to take responsibility for your own expansion of perception and to will this with intent. Intention requires attention of awareness and its focus. It is very likely that you who read this now will feel like an awakened dreamer in the land of the sleeping. You will look into the faces of those around you and see only the remnants of unconscious dreams. You shall walk amongst them with calm and humility – not arrogance or pride. All those awakened understand the plight of the sleepers, for they too were once asleep. Yet the sleeping dreamers can not yet appreciate those who are awakened for they are still asleep.

It may at times feel like a lonely Path. Yet it is also a Path of Family. You are all Family. Amongst yourselves as well as with others within the expanded expressions of consciousness. You are experiencing a life within a physical body in this present moment. Your life experiences are many. Your expressions of consciousness are many. After this life experience, you shall know that you are part of an expansive consciousness; and that here, you are only a localized expression of it. Trust that there is much more to experience, learn, and grow from. Make the best decisions that align with your inner sense. Allow your *own truths to guide you* and never feel you are alone. There is nothing to fear except your own fears.

Take the Path that speaks to you. If there are triggers needed to awaken you, consider these communications as one of them. Belong to your Self and own your opportunities and your accomplishments.

TWENTY TWO

Every individual being can gain awareness of the most appropriate way to live their life. You are each a bundle of awareness. Each step toward the comprehension of your truth is a step worth taking. The vastness of the life experience, and the immensity of the plans, agendas, and forces operating in your reality and upon this planet is staggering. It is staggering to human perception because such perceptions have been restricted for so long. It is time to work towards expanding your awareness. Humanity *must expand its awareness*, otherwise it will never accept the Greater Reality of what is going on.

Each time a person says 'I can't believe that,' it means they lack the capacity to approach something from beyond the confines of their conditioning. Evolvement and growth does not happen because of the 'I can't believe that' crowd. Creative intent, conscious awareness, and allowance, balance, and alignment are the forces that resonate with the life flows within the cosmos. The 'I can't believe that' crowd all remain in the pond, afraid to follow the tributary into the ocean. Those who remain in the pond pull each other back so that they all stay. Those that find the pathways into the ocean help one another along so that they all go.

Become your own diligence. There is no time left now in your life experience to say: 'But I didn't know.' Many are those who choose not to know. Many are those who choose not to question, to seek, or to uncover the many hidden truths. The contentment of the masses is no excuse for those who have awakened or are awakening. Some individuals change their classrooms during the life experience. And many do not.

Your Path is your own. Many pathways criss-cross, overlap, and meet upon the Way. Yet the Path is unique to you. That is why you must choose to own your truths, and not those of others. When you arrive at your door, only your own hand can open it. What then for all the talk and excuses of others?

Open your eyes to the Game of Life. Enjoy your participation and learn from each experience and encounter instead of saying this is 'bad' and that was 'good' and then feeling pleased or resentful. This is not YOU. Only by opening up your awareness to the possibilities and the potentials of so much more will the pathways then be opened up within you. Making the decisions that align you with yourself will also align you with the encouragement of the cosmos. How many more nudges do you need?

These communications likewise have their time and place and function. When they are done, they are done. The rest is for each of you to take forward in your own ways – by your own steps, or sometimes by joining in like-resonance with others for part of the journey. It is your discernment now that will decide your future steps. Discernment allows for experience, and experience allows for wisdom to be gained. With wisdom comes awareness. Awareness leads to expanded perception and the further expression of consciousness. You shall receive *in accordance with your will*.

Therefore, <u>will with conscious intent.</u>

Your physical body provides you with the hand. It is your conscious intent that must focus the hand to reach for the door of your Path.

Never forget that there are others like yourself. You may not know of one another, yet you exist as a vibrational Family. If you feel a strong need to, then seek them out, and share some physical time in company. If you find yourselves in difficult times, find and align with the roses and not the thorns. Choose your area of the garden carefully. From your place, keep your force of attention and awareness steady.

Stay Awake. Stay Aware.

Do not become disheartened, dear Friend.

Through the Work of owning your own truths, you shall find the pathways of your own meaning and purpose. These will bring you the energy you require for sustaining your path. This

164

energy cannot be found in the material things of the world. Genuine meaning transcends all earthly satisfactions. We encourage each of you now to find your own inner authority and to walk quietly through the world with this awareness and knowing. Share it and pass it on to others. Allow each other to find this personal freedom. Be committed to your Own Work.

There is a different Knowing awaiting to be known. It is a Knowing that enhances the evolvement of conscious awareness. There is meaning in everything, no matter the experiences that result. Remember: this is not about 'good' or 'bad' – it is about the allowance of evolvement and awareness. Sometimes it is necessary to be squeezed by uncomfortable forces in order to find the most appropriate release. Do not place the blame upon others. Instead, recognize that everything you are now going to experience is to allow you to come closer to your own Self. The moment is arriving where choices will become more necessary, as certain windows of opportunity are closing. These are the choices that shall allow you to grow with greater acceleration if you choose correctly. These are the choices that can be your own **human becoming.**

It is your time now to be responsible - and to think, feel, act, imagine, and intend with responsibility.

The stability and focused conscious awareness of the few will become the Family for the future. They shall hold the intensity of the energies to come. Those who can, must become.

The expansion of conscious awareness into this reality is in process. There is much that still needs to play out within this grand cosmic Game. It is impossible to give more indication, or to even give words. For this reason, we encourage each person to find what feels true to them by owning who they really are. Less of the self-delusions and more of the self-knowing. Those who quietly accomplish their parts are those that shall find the most encouragement. To 'hold the energy' whilst the ground shakes is no small accomplishment. Subtlety is your power, for true power is subtle.

Within these words, we give you our blessing and our encouragement. We appreciate all you have done, all that you do, and all that you shall accomplish. We recognize you and we are grateful. We are grateful for your service and your commitment to the Work. We are with You.

It is only by becoming closer to yourself

will you ever get closer to your truths.

ABOUT KSP

In the Heart of One

Is the Heart of All.

In the Space of One

Is the Space of All.

In the Being of One

Is the Being of All.

In You

Are We.

Made in the USA
Middletown, DE
30 July 2021